PEARSON
PUBLISHING

Revision Guide GCSE English and English Literature

James Durran and Jim Stewart

James Durran is an Advanced Skills Teacher at Parkside Community College in Cambridge.
Jim Stewart is Assistant Headteacher at St Peter's School in Huntingdon.

Cartoons by Steve Clarke

Hands off!

This book belongs to:

Name ....

Class ....

School ....

Date of exams..

Coursework deadline dates..

....

....

Exam board ....

Specification number ....

Candidate number...

Centre number ....

Further copies of this publication may be obtained from:

Pearson Publishing
Chesterton Mill, French's Road, Cambridge CB4 3NP
Tel 01223 350555 Fax 01223 356484
Email info@pearson.co.uk Web site www.pearsonpublishing.co.uk

ISBN: 1 85749 850 9

Published by Pearson Publishing 1999
© Pearson Publishing 1999
Fourth edition 2003

Contents

Introduction

— IF ONLY I'D REVISED!

*Although she'd never know it,
she was having an existential experience*

This guide is designed to help you to work effectively on your own as you prepare for the AQA (Specification A) exams in GCSE English and GCSE English Literature. It will not replace the work that you do in school with your English teacher, but it will help you to revise what you have learned during the GCSE course.

It will also help you to structure your revision and make the most efficient use of your time as you prepare for the exams. The activities are designed to help you to feel more confident about tackling the exams. They do this by helping you to see what you already know, and showing you how to make the best use of this knowledge.

What advice does the guide give?

The guide gives advice on:

- what the examiners are looking for
- revising and preparing for each section of the exams
- annotating your exam texts effectively
- practising planning and writing exam answers
- reading exam papers and understanding exactly what the questions are asking for
- planning and organising your time in the exams
- quoting effectively
- using technical terms effectively
- developing reading skills.

The guide starts with general advice, and there is then a separate section on each part of the English and English Literature exams.

There is also a guide to technical terms that you may find useful (see *Chapter 8*, page 87).

How can you use the guide?

 The guide suggests activities that will help you to revise and prepare for the exam. These are shown by this icon.

Some of the activities do not ask you to write much at all – just to think, to mark texts (where you are allowed to) and, perhaps, make a few notes. These will give you confidence that you do have things to write.

Some suggest very short pieces of writing, which will help you to write quickly and concisely, putting complicated ideas into a few words. This is a very important skill in the exam.

There are also some suggestions for longer pieces of writing to do – very useful if you have the time.

Many of the activities in the guide would also be suitable for you to work on with a friend, or in a group of friends. The discussion involved in sorting out your ideas will be very helpful. However, you should practise writing on your own, too.

Some of the activities are divided into easy, less easy and hard. You might want to start with the easy activities, and work your way through, or you may decide to start with the less easy or hard activities. You might want to ask your teacher to suggest which activities are best for you. The activities are shown by these icons:

 Easy   Less easy   Hard

The exam papers

AQA GCSE English (Specification A) Paper 1

Section A: Reading (One hour)

You will have to read and answer questions on some non-fiction and media texts that you have not seen before (see *Chapter 2*, page 9).

Section B: Writing to argue, persuade or advise (45 minutes)

You will have to do a piece of writing which does one or more of these things and which may be connected to the texts in Section A (see *Chapter 3*, page 22).

AQA GCSE English (Specification A) Paper 2

Section A: Reading (45 minutes)

You will have to write about the 'Poems from different cultures and traditions' you have studied in Section 1 of the AQA Anthology (see *Chapter 5*, page 46).

Section B: Writing to inform, explain or describe (45 minutes)

You will have to do a piece of writing which does one or more of these things (see *Chapter 4*, page 36).

AQA GCSE English Literature (Specification A)

Section A: Post-1914 Prose (45 minutes)

You will have to write about the novel or the short stories that you have studied (see *Chapters 6* and *7*, pages 59 and 73).

Section B: Pre-1914 and Post-1914 Poetry (one hour)

You will have to write about the poems in Section 2 of the Anthology (English Literature) (see *Chapter 5*, page 46).

1 General advice

The main sections of this chapter are:

- Looking back over your GCSE work
- Practising planning and writing
- The exam papers
- Reading exam questions
- Quoting.

Looking back over your GCSE work

Spend some time getting all your notes and other work into order, if you have not already done so.

Look back over the pieces of writing that you have done during the course, especially:

- Year 10 and 11 assignments
- exam practices
- mock exam answers.

Look at how your writing has developed. Look at the comments from your teacher.

You could make some quick notes on the following things:

- **Working in exam conditions** – What have you learned about what you need to improve in this? For example, do you read the questions carefully? Do you plan effectively? Do you spend the right amount of time on each question? There is lots of advice on this later in the guide.
- **Aspects of your writing** – What do you need to improve about the way that you write in exams? This includes all writing – about the Anthology, unseen texts, literature texts, and different kinds of original writing.
- **Technical accuracy** – Marks are given – and lost – in the exam for technical accuracy (spelling and punctuation) and presentation (including handwriting). What, exactly, do you need to improve?

He did not recall a single worksheet,
but he recognised the gum

Practising planning and writing

Planning

One very effective way of revising is to practise planning exam answers. Your teacher will give you sample questions to work on.

The plan you write might take the form of a flow diagram, showing the order of the points you will make. It might be a quick note of events to refer to, or pages of a novel to find quotations on. It might be a spider diagram, showing which examples or points you will refer to in each section of your essay. If you practise, you will find a method that works for you. This is an example of a useful, quick plan for an exam answer about symbolic objects in *Lord of the Flies*:

When practising, you could spend a long time planning carefully and thinking hard about what to include in your essay. However, you could just give yourself a few minutes, as though you are in the actual exam. That way, you can do several practice plans in a short time.

Writing

Practising writing parts of answers, or whole answers, is very valuable. You might even persuade your teacher to mark one or two.

- It is useful to practise writing just the beginnings of answers. Start with a quick plan and then write just the opening paragraph. You could take your time over this, thinking through how to make your opening as effective as possible. Alternatively, give yourself five minutes to practise writing under pressure.

- It is also very useful to practise whole timed answers: ask your teacher to give you some examples of questions. Give yourself exactly the amount of time you would have in the exam. Check that you know what this is. Start by making a quick plan or use one of the opening paragraphs that you have written.

"Could you just mark these…"

4

- As you are revising, try putting key ideas into words. For example, you might have an idea about a character, or an idea about what a writer is saying: experiment with expressing this idea in one short paragraph. Could you put it more clearly? Could you weave in a quotation?

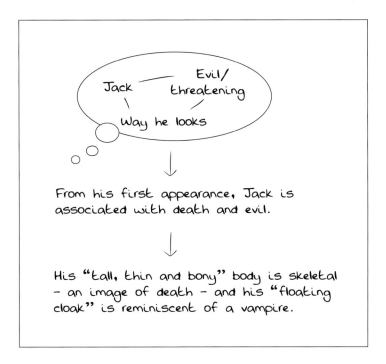

- Pick out an important phrase or sentence from a text you are revising. Try writing a sentence or two to explain the significance of this quotation: again, experiment with ways to make your explanation as clear as possible. Look at how this has been done in the example above.

The exam papers

To be well prepared, you need to know certain facts about the papers before you go into the exam room. These will include:

- how long each paper lasts
- how long you are expected to spend on each question
- what type of questions to expect on each paper and in each section (some are worth more marks than others)
- what particular skills each question is asking you to use
- whether you will need to write anything in rough and how long you should spend doing this
- what prepared texts you will be writing about and in which questions.

"But I hardly know you..."

Reading exam questions

The most important part of being successful in an exam is what might seem to be the simplest – answering what the question is asking. It is possible in the stress of exam conditions to misread or misunderstand the questions, but, with care, you can avoid this altogether.

As he raced to finish his second essay,
*he spotted the word **OR**…*

Chapter 9 (page 109) contains sample questions, annotated with advice and explanations of key words. Look through them carefully – but remember that the questions may not be exactly like these, as the way they are presented can change from year to year.

Some of the questions have bullet points, which are designed to help you think more deeply about what the question is asking for.

They also break the question down into smaller parts, to help you to structure your answer.

Read the advice about bullet points in *Chapter 8* (page 92).

Quoting

Using quotations well is a very effective way of improving your grades. It is important that you are confident about doing this.

There is advice in each chapter about making the best use of quotations for each section of the exam papers.

2 Reading unseen non-fiction and media texts

In **Section A** of **English Paper 1**, you will have to read and write about non-fiction and media texts that you have not seen before. There will be at least two texts. These might include newspaper or magazine articles, leaflets or advertisements, for example.

You will have prepared for and practised this in class. This chapter offers:

- advice about how to tackle the exam
- some ideas about what you should revise
- some suggestions for how you can do some more preparation on your own.

MAKES *16* LIGHT AND FLUFFY BUNS?

She was beginning to question whether this wasn't a work of fiction after all...

What the examiners are looking for

The following phrases may appear on the exam paper. You are being asked to:	These phrases mean you need to show that you can:
...distinguish between fact and opinion.	...tell the difference between fact and opinion.
...evaluate how information is presented.	...comment on how effectively the writer has presented ideas and information.
...follow an argument, identifying implications and inconsistencies.	...follow a writer's argument. ...recognise ideas in a text which are not stated directly. ...spot weaknesses in an argument (see page 15).
...select material appropriate to purpose.	...refer to and quote details in texts, which support your ideas.
...collate material from different sources.	...find and quote details from more than one text.
...make cross-references.	...compare texts, and how they have been written.
...read items as media texts.	...write confidently about images, layout and presentation (see page 16).

You will have to write about poems in Section 2 of the Anthology (English Literature) (see *Chapter 5*, page 46).

Tackling the exam paper

Reading the paper

This section tests your skills as a reader. When you open the paper you will find two or three non-fiction and media texts, which you will have to read and answer questions on.

It is very important that you read the questions before you read the texts. It would be a waste of time to read the texts first: you should be looking for particular ideas, features and information while you read.

Your first reading of the texts should be detailed. Use a pen, pencil or highlighter to mark useful points. You might:

- put a line in the margin next to a significant paragraph or sentence
- underline important phrases, or circle key words
- write words and phrases in the margin.

As you read, keep an eye on the questions. What do you need to look for?

For example:

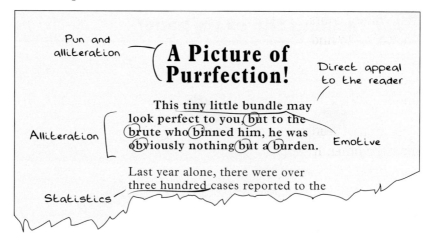

Chapter 9 (page 109) offers examples of questions, together with advice.

Timing

This section will be divided into several questions. It is very important that you look at how many marks there are for each. You should spend the most time, and write the most, on the question worth the highest number of marks.

Planning

For the longer questions, the examiners will be looking for evidence that you have put your ideas in order before starting to write. Make a quick list of points or a diagram of your ideas: do not just launch into the writing. For example, if you are comparing two texts, you might quickly make two lists – of similarities and of differences. The examiner will give marks for ideas shown in the plan, even if you do not have time to include them in your answer.

Writing in your own words

Even if you are asked to list points, you should put these in your own words as far as possible. To show that you understand what you have found, you may need to explain it.

Referring back to the texts

You will, of course, have to look back at the texts as you write your answers – to find information and examples, and to choose words and phrases to quote. You will not have time to reread the texts word for word. Your markings will help, but you will need to skim and scan the text, looking for key words and topics.

This kind of reading is not about reading individual words, one after the other. It is about looking at large chunks of text, and spotting particular words or ideas in them. You need to get used to looking at a whole page at a time. This involves moving your eyes quickly down the page, stopping at three or four points, and looking for key words or phrases.

 Practise this with a magazine or newspaper article. Read it once, then skim through it quickly looking for all the references to a particular person, place, or idea.

Checking and correcting

Leave yourself time to check your answers at the end.

 ## Checklists of ideas

The lists below are all ideas that you should be familiar with. You will need them when you are answering questions on the texts, writing about how effective they are, and especially when you are comparing texts with each other. Tick the ones you are confident about:

Language

- ☐ ambiguity
- ☐ assertion
- ☐ audience
- ☐ captions
- ☐ emotive language
- ☐ fact
- ☐ genre
- ☐ headline
- ☐ imperative
- ☐ narrative
- ☐ opinion
- ☐ persuasive language
- ☐ puns
- ☐ register
- ☐ repetition
- ☐ representation
- ☐ rhetorical questions
- ☐ symbolic

- ☐ sentence lengths
- ☐ slogan
- ☐ stereotype
- ☐ structure
- ☐ tone
- ☐ viewpoint
- ☐ voice

Layout and presentation

- ☐ bold type
- ☐ borders
- ☐ bullet points
- ☐ captions
- ☐ colour/black and white
- ☐ columns
- ☐ cross-heads
- ☐ frames
- ☐ font type and font size
- ☐ headline
- ☐ italic type
- ☐ justification
- ☐ logo
- ☐ mast-head
- ☐ pictures
- ☐ symbol
- ☐ text wrapping

Images

- ☐ background/foreground
- ☐ camera angle
- ☐ camera distance
- ☐ centre/margin
- ☐ colour/black and white
- ☐ cropping
- ☐ emotive
- ☐ frame
- ☐ left/right
- ☐ lighting
- ☐ medium (photograph/cartoon/drawing)
- ☐ mise-en-scène
- ☐ posture/expression/body language
- ☐ reading path
- ☐ symbolism
- ☐ viewpoint

Web sites and electronic texts

- ☐ animation
- ☐ banner
- ☐ button
- ☐ frames
- ☐ graphic
- ☐ hypertext
- ☐ icons
- ☐ link
- ☐ logo
- ☐ menu
- ☐ text
- ☐ thumbnail

There are lots of other features of language, that you are used to finding in poetry and stories but which might be in these texts as well. For example, imagery, metaphor, simile, alliteration, personification, onomatopoeia and so on. You will find explanations for many of these terms in *Chapter 8*.

Following an argument

In this section, you will be asked to follow a writer's argument. This will involve showing that you understand the points being made, and the ways in which the writer is making them. When revising for this section, look at some examples of argumentative writing.

Can you **identify** the writer's argument? This means understanding:

- the points they are making
- the reasons they are giving
- how these ideas have been put into a particular order.

Can you **analyse** the writer's technique? This means understanding how they are using:

- reasoning
- facts and statistics
- opinion
- other persuasive techniques (see page 29).

Can you **evaluate** the argument? This means saying how effective you think it is and why. How persuasive do you find the argument? Look for any weaknesses, such as:

- assertions without evidence
- contradictions
- only using facts and statistics which suit the argument
- faulty logic.

Fact and opinion

When following a writer's argument, or if you are asked to find particular information or ideas in a text, then it is essential that you can tell the difference between fact and opinion. (See *Chapter 8*, pages 94 and 100.)

Images, layout and presentation

In this section, you will be asked to write not only about the words in the texts, but the way in which they are presented on the page, and the way the page is laid out and the images chosen. When revising, look at examples of texts in which these things are important – magazine pages, leaflets or advertisements, for example.

Can you explain:

- how the layout and images make the messages or meanings in the text clearer or stronger?
- how they work together with (or against) the words?
- why particular images have been chosen, and the effects they are meant to have on the reader?
- how images and design features suggest ideas or feelings?

 ## Comparing texts

On this paper, you will be asked to compare two or more texts. Bullet points in the question will help. Make sure that you cover each point. You may be asked to write about how the texts are similar and how they are different in any of the following ways:

- What are the writers trying to do?
- How are the texts aimed at particular readers?
- How have the writers used language?
- How is each text presented on the page?
- How are images used in each text?
- How are the texts structured differently from each other?
- What is the tone of each text?
- How effective is each text?
- What is your response to each text and which do you prefer? (See *Planning* on page 12.)

The following words and phrases are useful for starting or joining sentences, when you are comparing texts:

Although...
In the first text...
Compared with...
While one text...

...in the other...
However,...
Nevertheless,...
...the second text...
On the other hand,...
In comparison,...
Meanwhile,...
In contrast,...
...whereas...
...while...
Similarly,...
Equally,...
In the same way...

Quoting

When you are writing about the non-fiction texts in the exam, it is very important that you quote from them. Well-chosen quotations show your understanding of the text and of the point that you are making. Although you cannot quote from a picture, you can describe it. For example:

Whereas the newspaper article presents facts, the leaflet tries to persuade the reader to agree with the protestors' point of view, and this is reflected in the language of both. The newspaper refers neutrally to "the building of the new road", which the leaflet describes emotively as leaving "a trail of destruction". The choice of pictures reinforces this contrast. The article is illustrated with a simple map, suggesting objectivity; the leaflet's images of small, appealing animals are highly emotive.

Quotation marks around any quoted words

Reference to details in layout and images

17

Practising planning and writing

One of the most effective ways to revise for this part of the exam is to get used to tackling the kinds of questions that are in the paper. Your teacher will give you examples of these to practise with. Look at the advice on *Practising planning and writing* in *Chapter 1*.

Newspaper article	Leaflet
More factual	More opinion
Neutral tone	Angry tone
More formal	More informal
Neutral language	Emotive language
More statistics	Statistics selected to support opinions
Informative map	Emotive images
Objective	Obviously biased
Impersonal, dull	Appeals directly to the reader
Longer sentences and paragraphs	Shorter sentences and paragraphs

 Other ways to prepare for this section

For some of the following activities, you will need some non-fiction texts to work with. You could use articles and reports from newspapers and magazines, information leaflets, advertisements, school brochures for parents, Web pages, CD-ROM pages, campaign leaflets, holiday brochures, etc.

His preparation had bin excellent

Every time you read a newspaper, magazine, leaflet or advertisement, think about who it is aimed at, and how it has been written with that audience in mind. Look at the language that is being used.

• • • • •

Collect some of these non-fiction texts. Divide them into ones which are mainly about getting information across, and ones which try to persuade the reader to do or think something. Then look again at the information texts. Can you find anything in them which is, in fact, meant to be persuasive?

• • • • •

Choose a text which has an argument in it – an attempt to persuade the reader to think or feel in the same way as the writer. Go through it and underline what you think are the four main points that the writer is making. You could then try summarising the argument in your own writing, in no more than 50 words.

Look at the same text. In one colour, underline any facts; in another colour, underline any opinions. Can you explain which opinions are implicit, and which are explicit? (See page 100.)

Look at the same text again. Think about how effective this writer's arguments are. Which part of their argument do you think is most effective? Try to explain why in writing, using no more than 40 words. Which part of their argument do you think is least effective? Try to explain why in writing, using no more than 40 words. Remember to quote words and phrases from the text.

• • • • •

Take two or three texts of different kinds. Try to find just one example of each of the things in the following list:
- bullet points
- emotive language
- fact
- effective or unusual layout
- opinion
- persuasive language
- repetition, used for effect
- a rhetorical question
- a slogan
- a stereotype
- a picture intended to play on the reader's emotions
- a clear voice coming through the text
- short sentences, used for effect
- a strong image.

• • • • •

Look for two different texts about the same thing. For example, they might be two different newspaper reports on the same event, or a magazine article and a newspaper report on the same topic. Make a list of similarities and differences between the two texts. You could use this checklist to help you:
- ☐ What are the writers trying to do?
- ☐ How are the texts aimed at particular readers?
- ☐ How have the writers used language?
- ☐ How is each text presented on the page?
- ☐ How are images used in each text?

☐ How are the texts structured differently from each other?
☐ What is the tone of each text?
☐ How effective is each text?
☐ What is your response to each text and which do you prefer?

• • • • •

Find a persuasive or argumentative text. Try to find three facts. Then try to find three opinions. Can you find an opinion that is presented as though it was a fact?

• • • • •

With the same or a different text, go through and highlight all the emotive words. What is their overall effect?

• • • • •

"Read it to me one last time before I go ..."

Look through a magazine, and find all the advertisements in which images are important. Would you be able to explain why each image has been chosen? Try to think of one word to describe the effect of each image as precisely as possible.

Choose just one of the advertisements. Write down four words to describe the feelings that this image gives you. Now try writing a sentence to describe the effect of the image.

• • • • •

Browse some different Web sites, and make sure that you can identify examples of the design features listed on page 14. Can you describe the effect of each? Do they make pages easier to read or to interact with? How do they add to the impact of the page and how it looks?

3 Writing to argue, persuade or advise

In **Section B** of **English Paper 1**, you will have to produce a piece of writing which will be related to what you have been reading and writing about in Section A of the same paper. There will be four tasks, from which you will have to choose one. This will involve arguing, persuading or advising, or a mixture of these.

Arguing

means expressing a point of view as clearly and effectively as possible. It will usually involve presenting evidence and a series of reasons.

Persuading

means getting your readers to agree with a point of view or to feel something. It might involve argument, but it will usually also involve other methods of trying to affect people's feelings about something.

Advising

means suggesting how somebody might do something, or how they might solve a problem.

You will have prepared for and practised this in class. This chapter does not attempt to teach you how to do these kinds of writing, but it does offer:

- advice about how to tackle the exam
- some ideas about what you should revise
- some suggestions for how you can do some more preparation on your own.

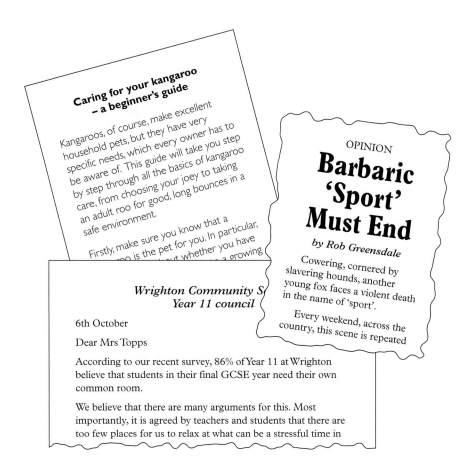

Caring for your kangaroo – a beginner's guide

Kangaroos, of course, make excellent household pets, but they have very specific needs, which every owner has to be aware of. This guide will take you step by step through all the basics of kangaroo care, from choosing your joey to taking an adult roo for good, long bounces in a safe environment.

Firstly, make sure you know that a ～ is the pet for you. In particular, ～ whether you have ～growing

OPINION

Barbaric 'Sport' Must End

by Rob Greensdale

Cowering, cornered by slavering hounds, another young fox faces a violent death in the name of 'sport'.

Every weekend, across the country, this scene is repeated

Wrighton Community S￼
Year 11 council

6th October

Dear Mrs Topps

According to our recent survey, 86% of Year 11 at Wrighton believe that students in their final GCSE year need their own common room.

We believe that there are many arguments for this. Most importantly, it is agreed by teachers and students that there are too few places for us to relax at what can be a stressful time in

What the examiners are looking for

✓ Can you communicate clearly in writing?

✓ Can you write for a particular audience?

✓ Can you write for a particular purpose?

✓ Can you use a wide and appropriate vocabulary?

✓ Can you select and use information effectively?

✓ Can you organise ideas into sentences, paragraphs and whole texts?

✓ Can you spell accurately?

✓ Can you punctuate accurately?

✓ Can you use Standard English when appropriate?

✓ Can you present work neatly and clearly?

✓ Is your handwriting clear and readable?

Unfortunately, her vocabulary was now so wide she couldn't get it through the exam room door...

Tackling the exam paper

Reading the paper

It is very important that you read all of the questions carefully
before deciding which to answer. You need to think about the
type, or types, of writing that each question asks for, and decide
which one you can do best. For example, you may have a choice of
writing a magazine article, a letter, or an advice sheet. By now, you
should know which type of writing will give you the chance to do
your best work – and this will almost certainly be the one
to choose.

In *Chapter 9* (page 109), there are examples of questions, together
with advice.

Planning and writing

You will be given advice at the beginning of Section B about how to
spend the time that is allowed for the question. This will probably
suggest that you spend five minutes planning and then five minutes
checking and correcting what you have written. It is very important
that you follow this advice about time.

The examiners will be looking for evidence that you have put your
ideas in order before starting to write. Make a list of points or a
diagram of your ideas. Careful planning is essential: do not just
launch into the writing. The examiner will give marks for ideas
shown in the plan, even if you do not have time to include them in
your answer. Look at the example on page 27.

It is vital that you think very carefully about the purpose and the
audience of the piece of writing. The examiners will be looking for
evidence that you have done this.

Make sure that you write enough. Often, people lose marks on this
section by writing too little. For example, a letter less than a side
long is not enough for 45 minutes' writing. However, more than
two sides is likely to be too much.

Presentation

If you are writing a letter, a leaflet or a feature for a magazine, then the way it is laid out or presented will matter. However, you should not spend too long on this: the words are the most important thing.

Make sure that you revise how to set out formal and informal letters.

Checking and correcting

Remember that this is one of the sections in the exam where you can gain or lose marks for spelling, punctuation, grammar and presentation.

Leave yourself time to check your answers at the end. Five minutes should be enough. For example:

Look for repeated words

Look for missing capitals

Look for spelling mistakes

must stop. In our our society
excuse for such a barbaric s
as this.
furthermore, research
90% support the complete
mediately. Surely, this mus
rabbits.
However the so-called i
expect us to believe that thi

Practising planning and writing

Practising the kinds of questions that are in the paper is one of the most effective ways to prepare for this part of the exam. Ask your teacher for examples to work on. Remember to check the advice on *Practising planning and writing* in *Chapter 1*.

For this section of the exam, it can be particularly useful to practise writing just the beginnings of answers. Look at the examples on page 23.

If you are writing an argument, then planning is especially important as you will be assessed on the way you develop your points.

Below is a useful structure:

Start strongly – perhaps with a striking *fact*,
or a *rhetorical* question.

Plan a series of points, which build to a
concluding paragraph.

Always support opinions and ideas with facts,
and comment on the facts you choose, ie:

comment/opinion
fact
comment/opinion
fact
comment/opinion
(and so on)

Keep your paragraphs and sentences short
and easy to follow. This will help the reader to
understand your point.

End with another striking fact, a
direct appeal to the reader, or a
strong *rhetorical* question.

*Apparently, "Do I look stupid?" had
been a rhetorical question...*

Argumentative and persuasive writing: Useful techniques

Assertion	It is obvious that...
Emotive language, to arouse the reader's feelings	... terrible... charming... cruel... beautiful... appalling... abandoned... lost... little...
Facts or evidence, to support an argument	It is quite legal to... For example...
Giving reasons	If... then... It is clear from... that...
Commentary, to explain how the facts support your point of view	Facts such as this show...
Statistics	In 2002, 12,000 animals were used in...
Clearly-stated opinions	I believe that this is completely wrong, and...
Repetition of words or phrases, to emphasise ideas and points	These animals suffer, these animals are put through torment, and these animals die, so that our eyes won't sting if we get shampoo in them.
Rhetorical questions	Is this the behaviour we expect of a civilised society?
A strong voice	This must end.
Appealing to the reader directly	You may think that... You too can... Next time you...

Argumentative and persuasive writing: Useful words and phrases

Listing points	First(ly)…
	Secondly,… etc.
Giving examples	For example,…
	… such as…
	… as shown by…
Reasoning logically	If… then…
	It is clear from… that…
Adding examples or points	… also…
	In the same way…
	As with…
	What's more,…
	Furthermore,…
Developing points	… because/as…
	Consequently,…
	Therefore…
	Since…
	In fact…
Emphasising a point	In particular,…
	Significantly,…
	Specifically,…
	… especially…
	Above all,…
Arguing against another point of view	However…
	Although…
	Nevertheless…
	Despite this…
	On the other hand…
	Whereas…
Making something seem obvious	Clearly…
	… of course…
	Naturally…
	Obviously…
	Surely…
	Certainly…
Concluding	On the whole…
	Finally…
	In conclusion…

Presenting two sides of a discussion: Useful phrases

On the one hand...

On the other...

It could be said that...

However, it could also be said that...

One point of view is that...

Alternatively...

There is some evidence that...

Equally, there is some evidence that...

Some people feel strongly that...

Despite this...

Whereas many people feel...

...others feel...

It could be argued...

Nevertheless...

Even without language she could be pretty persuasive…

Writing to advise: Useful words and phrases

Getting started

You will need...
Before you start...
First of all...

Advice

You should...
You could...
In order to...
So that...
You might...
You will probably...
Perhaps you could...
If... then...

Making time clear

First(ly)...
Secondly..., etc
Having...
Meanwhile...
Whenever...
When you have...
Eventually...
Finally...

Emphasising particular ideas

It is important to...
It is essential that...
... more important...
... especially...
Above all...
Remember...
Don't forget...
Of course...
Take care that...
Make sure that...
Always...

Other ways to prepare for this section

Preparation that you do for Section A of this paper (thinking about how writers write for particular purposes and audiences) is also important preparation for this section.

She probably wouldn't need it but she had everything else...

Writing an argument

 To practise putting together an argument, make a list of points (in any order) that you would use if you were doing one of the following tasks:

Either

- Write a letter to the headteacher of your school, arguing that Year 11 should have their own common room.

Or

- Write a speech to deliver to the rest of Year 11, arguing that they should each donate ten pounds towards buying furniture for the new Year 11 common room.

Now think about the order in which you put these points. Your first and last points will be particularly important. Also, you need to think carefully about the evidence that you will use to support your argument.

Go through the list of words on page 30 and pick out one word from each group that would make an argument sound more formal. For example, if you were writing for your headteacher, or trying to sound knowledgeable to the public, you might write "furthermore...", rather than "what's more...". (See **Register** in *Chapter 8*, page 103.)

Now try writing your argument in no more than 200 words. (This is less than you should write in the exam.) As you write, use the words in the list to help you structure your argument, and to help you make it sound convincing.

Writing persuasively

 To practise writing persuasively, try one of the following, in no more than 200 words. (This is less than you should write in the exam.)

Either

• Write a leaflet to distribute to the public, putting forward your point of view about a controversial topic, such as drugs, euthanasia, hunting, boxing or gun control.

Or

• Imagine that an area of park or countryside near your home is going to be destroyed to build a new road. Write a letter to a newspaper, either trying to persuade readers that this is a good idea, or trying to persuade them that it is a bad idea.

Before you start, though, look at the list of techniques on page 29. Think carefully about how you could use them in your own writing.

When you have finished, look back at what you have written and see how many of the techniques you have used. How effective are they? How well have you fitted your writing to your audience?

It is worth having this list of techniques in your mind as a sort of checklist for the exam.

Try one of the following tasks, writing no more than 200 words. (This is less than you should write in the exam.)

Either

- Your school magazine has a regular feature about people's hobbies and interests, aimed at beginners who want to know more. Write an introduction to one of your hobbies or interests, advising a beginner about the best ways in which to get started.

Or

- Write an advice sheet for Year 10 students who are about to start studying English GCSE. This should include advice on the best ways for students to:
  - manage their time
  - organise their written work
  - make the best of coursework
  - prepare for exams.

Before you start, think carefully about how you can lay the advice out to make it as clear as possible.

As you write, use the list of words on page 32 to help you.

When you have finished, look back over your advice. Could it have been clearer? How?

Remember that the task you choose in the exam may involve arguing, persuading and advising all at once.

He felt he needed better advice to complete the task

4 Writing to inform, explain or describe

In **Section B** of **English Paper 2**, you will have to produce a piece of writing. There will be a choice of four tasks, from which you will have to choose one. This will involve informing, explaining or describing, or a mixture of these.

Informing

means putting information across as clearly and understandably as possible.

"…she WHAT?!"

Explaining

means helping your readers to understand an idea or a point of view.

Describing

means putting across what something is like in an imaginative way.

After four hours she was confirmed as the world's worst charades player…

You will already have practised these kinds of writing in class. This chapter does not attempt to teach you how to do these kinds of writing, but it does offer:

- advice about how to tackle the exam
- some ideas as to what you should revise
- some suggestions for how you can do more preparation on your own.

I Remember...

Although I didn't know it at the time, that sunny Wednesday morning was going to be a turn in my life.

Let me explain.

Every Wednesday at St Olaf's Primary started the same way – assembly with and the rabbits' little

The Forth Railway Bridge

Over the grey, blustery Firth towers the awe-inspiring bridge, as it has for over a hundred years. For over a over a hundred years this rugged structure of ed y has carried trains going the Highlands, above the

Wrighton Community School
Student Prospectus

You've read the official prospectus: here's the real story!

We've been here for almost five years now, longer than a lot of the teachers have, so we think we've got a few things to tell you. Over the next few pages, you'll find all the information you need to survive at Wrighton.

Before we start though, let's get something straight. The most important thing that you need to know about being here is that

What the examiners are looking for

✓ Can you communicate clearly in writing?

✓ Can you write for a particular audience?

✓ Can you write for a particular purpose?

✓ Can you use a wide and appropriate vocabulary?

✓ Can you select and use information effectively?

✓ Can you organise ideas into sentences, paragraphs and whole texts?

✓ Can you spell accurately?

✓ Can you punctuate accurately?

✓ Can you use Standard English when appropriate?

✓ Can you present work neatly and clearly?

✓ Is your handwriting clear and readable?

Tackling the exam paper

Reading the paper

It is very important that you read all of the questions carefully before deciding which to answer. Remember that this section tests your skills as a writer. Think about the type, or types, of writing that each question asks for, and which ones you can do best. Which type of writing will give you the chance to do your best work?

In *Chapter 9* (page 109), there are examples of questions, together with advice.

Planning and writing

At the beginning of Section B there will be advice about how to spend the time that is allowed for the question. You should spend five minutes planning and then five minutes checking and correcting what you have written. It is essential that you use your time efficiently.

The examiners will be looking for evidence that you have put your ideas into order before starting to write. Make a list of points or a diagram of your ideas. Remember that you will be expected to write at least two sides in your answer. Careful planning is essential: don't just launch into the writing. The examiner will give marks for ideas shown in the plan, even if you do not have time to include them in your answer. Look at the example on page 41.

It is important that you think very carefully about the purpose of the piece of writing and the audience.

The most important thing here is to write something interesting, and to write in an imaginative and inventive way. Do not just string facts together: be personal – try to surprise, entertain, unsettle, intrigue or otherwise interest the reader. Find an original way of starting your piece of writing.

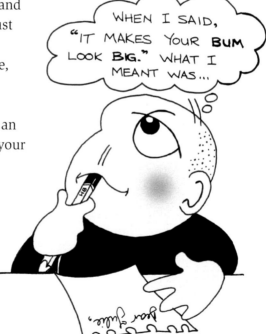

Whatever you write, do not do a rough draft – you will not have time.

Make sure that you write enough. The examiners will be looking for evidence that you can sustain a piece of writing (keep it going), so something very short won't do, however brilliantly it is written. Aim to write between one and two sides.

Real or imaginary?

A question might ask you to write about yourself – about an incident, a memory, or a place you know, for example. What you write about could be real or made up. You may feel more comfortable making something up, and you may be able to make it more interesting; on the other hand, people often write very well about real things, as they have more to say and have real feelings and thoughts to express.

Presentation

In some pieces of writing – a letter, for example – the way it is laid out or presented matters. However, you should not spend too long on this: the words are the most important thing.

Checking and correcting

Remember that this is one of the sections in the exam where you can gain or lose marks for spelling, punctuation, grammar and presentation.

Leave yourself time to check your answers at the end.

Practising planning and writing

One of the best ways to prepare for this part of the exam is to have a go at the kinds of questions that are in the paper. Ask your teacher for examples of these to practise with. Look at the advice on *Practising planning and writing* in *Chapter 1*.

Surviving GCSE – a leaflet

1 Make up quotations from students
2 Introduction: how leaflet will help
3 The work   – lessons
                      – homework
                      – practicals
                      – coursework   written   what to expect, and what teachers expect
                      – exams   oral
                                             practical
4 Using time   – deadlines
                      – independent study
5 Starting the course
                      – organisation
                      – things you will need

For this section of the exam, it can be particularly useful to practise writing the beginnings of texts which inform, explain or describe. How can you make an impact straight away? How can you grab your reader's attention? Look at the examples on page 37.

Useful words and phrases for starting and joining sentences

Explaining why	... because...
	... as...
	Consequently...
	Therefore...
	Since...
	... so...
	As a result...
Putting ideas into order	First(ly)...
	Secondly... etc.
	Next...
	... then...
	... as long as...
	Meanwhile...
	Whenever...
	Eventually...
	Finally...
	... after(wards)...
Developing ideas	What is more...
	In addition...
Giving examples	For example...
	... such as...
	... suggested by...
Comparing ideas and examples	Equally...
	Similarly...
	In the same way...
	As with...
	Likewise...
	Again...
	However...
	Although...
	Nevertheless...
	Despite this...
	Alternatively...
	On the other hand...
	Whereas...
	Compared to...
Emphasising ideas	In particular...
	... more important...
	Significantly...
	Specifically...
	... especially...
	Above all...
Concluding	In brief...
	On the whole...
	To sum up...
	In conclusion...

Other ways to prepare for this section

 Choose one of the following sample questions:

Either

- Write an introduction to an unofficial school prospectus, informing new pupils at your school about what the school is really like.

Or

- Write about an important and memorable event in your life. Explain what happened and why it was significant to you.

Or

- Describe a place that you can remember well from when you were younger. For example, a house you lived in, a place you went to on holiday, or a place where you used to play when you were small. It could be real or imaginary.

● ● ● ● ●

 Pick one question and write down ten key words that you might use in your answer. Decide which three words from your list are the most important. Then decide which one word is most important. For example:

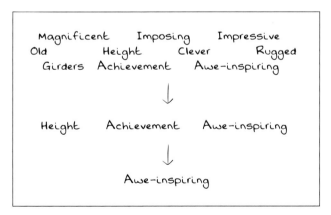

This sort of quick gathering of ideas and language can be very useful, and can give you confidence as you start to write.

43

Look back at your words. Can you replace any of them with more interesting words?

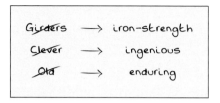

Now do this for the other two questions.

Look at your three lists. Are you choosing different sorts of words for the different sorts of task?

• • • • •

 Look at the beginnings of some stories or novels – just the opening paragraphs. Which one do you think is the most effective? What has the writer done to grab your attention or interest? Look for examples of mystery, shock, surprise, strangeness, putting the reader in the middle of a story, and other techniques.

Now try using one of these methods to write the opening paragraph of a practice answer. Does it help you to get started?

It is important to make your opening as effective as you can. Never start in an obvious way: start in the middle, or with something that will puzzle or shock the reader.

Now he had the examiner's attention...

• • • • •

 This is a good way of practising descriptive writing.

Imagine a place you know well, or an imaginary place. It could be any sort of place – beautiful, hostile, mysterious or ordinary. Get a picture of it in your mind and hold that picture for a few seconds.

Now quickly write down:

- three colours that you can see in the scene
- three shapes that you can see
- three textures that you can 'see' (eg 'spiky' or 'polished')
- three sounds that you can imagine in the scene
- three smells that you can imagine in the scene
- three feelings that you can sense in the scene ('gloom', 'joy' or 'anger')
- three metaphors to describe parts of the scene (for example, a tree might look like a crane, or a river might seem like a stream of blood).

Then try to write a description of the scene, weaving these ideas together. Experiment with mixing the different senses and feelings together, to create unusual descriptions: "spiky blue"; "dazzling bird-song"; "angry, orange light". Give yourself a time limit: it could be the full hour, or you could work for just 20 minutes, and see how much you can write.

Reread your description. How could you improve it?

• • • • •

Choosing the right words can help you to suit your writing to your audience. Go through the list on page 42 and pick out five words that would make an explanation sound more formal. For example, if you were writing formally, you might write "In conclusion...", rather than "To sum up...".

• • • • •

Now try writing a short, formal letter (no more than 150 words) to a fast food restaurant. You are complaining that you found a human ear in your meal and you would like a refund. You need to explain what has happened and what you want to be done. In your letter, try to include formal words from the list. Remember to set your letter out correctly.

• • • • •

Note that the task you choose in the exam may involve informing, explaining and describing all at once.

45

5 Revising a collection of poems

English Paper 2, Section A

You will have to write for 45 minutes about the 'Poems from different cultures and traditions' which you have studied in the AQA Anthology. This essay counts for 15% of your total English mark.

English Literature Paper, Section B

You will have to write for one hour about the other poems which you have studied from the AQA Anthology – the pre-1914 poems, and poems by either Seamus Heaney and Gillian Clarke, or Carol Ann Duffy and Simon Armitage. This essay counts for 40% of your total English Literature mark, which is more than all of your Literature coursework put together, so it is worth putting considerable time into revising for it.

In the exams, you will be expected to compare poems. This chapter will help you to do this, by revising poems together, not on their own.

 What the examiners are looking for

✓ Do you know the poems well?
✓ Do you understand how the writers have used language and form to create effects, and can you refer to particular examples?
✓ Can you say what you think poems mean or are about?
✓ Can you compare poems? This will usually mean comparing two, three or four poems.
✓ Can you make your personal response to the poems clear? This means showing that you have thought about them, and that you have ideas and reactions of your own; it might mean writing about what you liked or disliked about them, too.

✓ Can you show understanding of social, cultural and historical context and literary traditions? (See page 52.)

✓ Can you quote and refer to details in the poems, to support your ideas?

 ## Comparing the poems

One of the main things that the examiners are looking for in these sections of the exam is your ability to compare texts. You will be writing about two, three or four poems in each section, and you must show that you are aware of how they are similar (in the way they are written and in what they are saying) and how they are different.

You should plan carefully for this: the bullet points in the question may help you with this. For example:

	Half Caste	Presents from my Aunts in Pakistan
Poets' ideas about who they are	• a whole person (misunderstood)	• difficult to define her identity (" ...no fixed nationality")
What they feel about who they are	• proud, defiant	• uncertain, confused, wanting to belong
The methods they use to reveal their ideas and feelings	• direct challenge to the reader • irony and sarcasm • seeming to put himself down • own voice (patois, accent written phonetically)	• teenage memories • drifting lines, reflecting lack of certainty • symbolism (eg "fretwork") • vivid description (eg colours) • culture represented by clothing

The following words and phrases are useful for starting or joining sentences, when you are comparing texts:

Although...

In the first text...

Compared with...

While one text...

...in the other...

However,...

Nevertheless,...

...the second text...

On the other hand,...

In comparison,...

Meanwhile,...

In contrast,...

...whereas...

...while...

Similarly,...

Equally,...

In the same way...

Tackling the exam paper

Reading the paper

Poems from different cultures and traditions (English paper 2, Section A)

There will be a choice of two questions, each asking you to write about a particular, named poem and to compare it with others. You will probably have studied only one of these named poems, so that will be the question that you answer.

If you know the poems named in both questions, then you have a choice. Read both questions carefully, and decide which one will allow you to write in the most interesting way.

Pre-1914 and post-1914 poetry
(English Literature paper, Section B)

Find the questions about the poets that you have studied –
Seamus Heaney and Gillian Clarke, or Carol Ann Duffy and
Simon Armitage. There will be a choice of three questions on
each pair of poets. You will have to write about four poems: one
poem by each of the two poets, and two poems from the pre-1914
Poetry Bank. Read the questions carefully: which one will give
you the best opportunity to show what you know? A question
may look hard, but it may encourage you to think and write in
interesting ways.

Planning

The examiners will be looking for evidence that you have organised
your ideas before writing. Make a quick list of points or a diagram
of your ideas: don't just start writing. Remember, though, that
in English Paper 2, Section A, you only have 45 minutes to write
about each set of poems, so your planning needs to be quick. (See
the section on *Practising planning and writing*, page 53.)

Referring back to the poems

You will, of course, have to look back at the poems before and as
you write your answers – to help you to plan your answer, to find
ideas and examples to refer to, and to choose words and phrases
to quote.

The activities below will help you to practise finding things in the
poems quickly, but you will need to know your way around them
very well. If you are taking the exam in 2004, you are allowed to
annotate the poems. (See *Annotating the text*, page 51.)

Technical terms

When you are writing about the poems, you should be able to
show your knowledge of technical terms, such as alliteration,
metaphor and so on. However, it is very important that you show
your understanding of how the writer has used these techniques to
create effects. Just spotting and listing them is not enough – in fact,
it may lose you marks.

Checking and correcting

Leave yourself a few minutes to check your answers at the end.
For example:

You can add extra bits in the margin, or at the end.

of the poem.

There are examples of t
alliteration, and other devic
soggy sands." *The repeated
watery sound. Also, the poe
rabbits.

Similarly, the poem "Z
rhythms of everyday speech,
images of dampness and dec

* and the
description
of the
pond at
twilight.

 ## Beginning your revision

You can do the following for each of the collections of poems that
you are revising:

- Reread the poems that you have studied.
- Look back over all the notes that you have made or been
  given when you studied the poems, and make sure that you
  understand them. You need to know about the main ideas in
  each poem.
- It is essential that
  you know how
  the poems can
  be compared and
  connected with
  each other. This is
  something that you
  will have worked
  on in class.

*"I'm telling you
the poems are
connected..."*

Annotating the text (2004 exam only)

It is very important that key ideas about the poems are at your fingertips in the exam. Mark key points and ideas. Underline useful quotations, or mark them in the margin. Concentrate on material to do with the main ideas or aspects of the poems that you have looked at. The process of doing the annotation is very good revision in itself.

Do not forget the rules about annotation: you are not allowed to write more than one or two words at a time in the margin. Your teacher will be able to tell you whether you have annotated too much.

The examiners will know immediately if you are just copying annotations from your text. Doing this will not get you marks. Make sure that you are thinking about and answering the question, in your own words, and that you are getting across your response to the poems.

Social, historical and cultural context

When you write about the 'Poems from different cultures and traditions' be prepared to refer to the cultures which the poems reflect.

In the other groups of poems, the examiners will still be looking for evidence that you are aware of the time and place in which a poem was written, and about what mattered to people then or there.

If a poem was written some time ago:
• how does it reflect the way people thought at the time, or what they valued?
• how does it relate to the history of the time?

If a poem is from a particular country, or a particular culture, how is this reflected in the way it is written, or in its ideas?

You will have discussed this when you studied the poems and it is worth reminding yourself about it now.

You will not need to write about this at length in the exam, and not for every poem, but you should try to show that you are aware of it, even if that only means writing a sentence or two. The examiners will not be impressed by pages of background information – they want you to show what you know about the poems.

 ## Quoting

When you are writing about the poems in the exam, it is important that you quote to support the points that you make in the essay. Well-chosen quotations show your knowledge of the poems. They also show that you understand the points that you are making. There are particular rules and conventions for quoting poetry. One of the most important is that you set out the lines as they are in the poem.

For example:

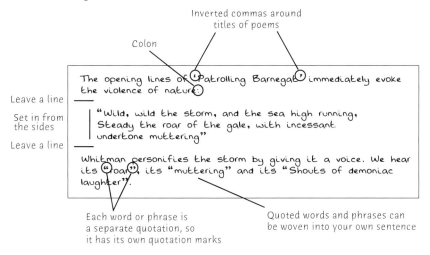

Colon

Inverted commas around titles of poems

Leave a line

Set in from the sides

Leave a line

The opening lines of "Patrolling Barnegat" immediately evoke the violence of nature:

"Wild, wild the storm, and the sea high running, Steady the roar of the gale, with incessant undertone muttering"

Whitman personifies the storm by giving it a voice. We hear its "roar", its "muttering" and its "Shouts of demoniac laughter".

Each word or phrase is a separate quotation, so it has its own quotation marks

Quoted words and phrases can be woven into your own sentence

Quotations should be brief and should not dominate the essay. As a rough guide, they should not take up any more than about 15% of the essay. Never quote more than two or three lines.

Practising planning and writing

To revise for these parts of the exam it is very helpful to get used to tackling the kinds of questions that are in the paper. Ask your teacher for examples of these to practise with. Look at the advice on *Practising planning and writing* in *Chapter 1*, and the example on page 47.

Other ways to revise a collection of poems

You can do the tasks over the page for each of the collections of poems that you are revising.

Thinking about the poems

These activities are designed to help you to find your way around the poems, to make connections between them, to practise selecting quotations, and to show you that you do know a lot about the poems as a group. Most of them can be done very quickly. Choose two or three activities to do in depth.

• • • • •

Write down the titles of the poems that you are revising. Around each, make some notes on what the title relates to in the poem. What ideas does it bring to mind? What feelings does it suggest?

• • • • •

Take one poem and try to sum up what it is about in five of your own words. Then sum it up in just one word. For example:

> Waste Boredom Regret
> Longing Frustration
>
> ↓
>
> Emptiness

• • • • •

Try this for the other poems. Look at the words together. Are there any connections?

I... HAVEN'T... GOT... A... CLUE!

Five words came instantly to mind...

• • • • •

Take one poem. Write down what you think is the most important line. Why did you choose this line?

Now pick out and write down what you think is the most important word in the line. Why did you choose it?

• • • • •

 Take one poem, write down six key images (word pictures). Why did you choose these images?

Then select what you think is the most important image in the poem. What makes it important?

Now try this for the other poems. Is it easier for particular kinds of poem?

• • • • •

 Pick one poem. Look at the first word. What does it tell you about the poem? Look at the last word. How does it leave the reader?

Then look at the first line and the last line. What is the effect of each?

Now do this for the other poems in the collection.

• • • • •

 Look at a group of poems by one poet. Write down the first word of each poem. Look at these words together. Are there any patterns which might tell you something about the group of poems?

• • • • •

 Pick a poem. Make a list of all the emotions that are in the poem. These might be in the experiences of any characters, in your own response to it, in the mind of the poet, or as suggested in the language in some way. Then write one or two words or phrases from the poem for each emotion.

For example:

· · · · ·

Do this for any other poems by the same author. What connections are there between the lists?

· · · · ·

Pick a theme that occurs in more than one of the poems in the group. It might be something like family, memory, childhood, nature, innocence and experience, environment, religion, community or difference.

Write down which poems relate to it.

Then choose and write down three or four quotations from each poem, that you might use if you were writing about this theme. Next to each quotation, you could write a few notes on how it relates to the theme.

What is different about the way the writers have dealt with this theme?

· · · · ·

Pick three poems by the same poet. Make a list of similarities in the way they are written – in the use of language, the structure, the voice behind the poem, and so on. Then make a list of themes or ideas that you can find in all three poems, and a list of words or images that are in all three poems.

You will find that there is lots to connect the poems, but you also need to think about differences. Write down two things about each poem that make it different from the others.

Which poem do you prefer? Why?

After ten minutes he had picked plenty... but nothing he felt he could write about...

•　•　•　•　•

Take a poem by one of the poets that you have studied for the English Literature paper, Section B. Then choose one of the poems that you have studied from the pre-1914 Poetry Bank, which seems connected to it in some way. They might be about a similar theme or subject, or be written in a similar form.

Use the list of connecting words and phrases on page 48 to practise writing sentences which compare the two poems – how are they similar and how are they different?

Try this with other poems by the two poets you have studied.

•　•　•　•　•

Choose two poems from the 'Poems from different cultures and traditions', which seem to be connected in some way. Use the list of connecting words and phrases on page 48 to practise writing sentences which compare the two poems – how are they similar and how are they different?

Writing about the poems

These activities will give you practice at writing in a concise and focused way.

•   •   •   •   •

 Imagine that you have been asked to read out three poems at an assembly for Year 9 pupils. The poems must be connected in some way.

Choose three of the poems you have studied and write a brief introduction to them (100 to 150 words), explaining what each one is about and what the connections are between them. What do you want your audience to listen out for particularly? What ideas or questions do the poems raise?

•   •   •   •   •

Take two or three poems that can be compared in an interesting way. Write between 150 and 200 words comparing the poems. You could write about the way the writers have used language, the ideas or themes in the poem, and your response to each one. Remember to write about things that are similar and things that are different.

•   •   •   •   •

This is a further activity for the 'Poems from different cultures and traditions'. You must think about the culture that is reflected in each poem. One of the questions may be about this, but, even if you answer the other question, you should try to refer to culture.

Take one poem. What can you tell about the culture that the poem shows or reflects? What can you tell about the way the poet relates to that culture? How does the poem draw on cultural experiences or knowledge that you are unfamiliar with? How else does the writing of the poem reflect a 'different' culture?

Revising a novel

In **Section A** of the **English Literature Paper**, you will have to write for 45 minutes either about a novel that you have studied, or about the short stories in the AQA Anthology. Remember that this one essay counts for 30% of the total English Literature mark, which is as much as all your Literature coursework put together, so it is worth putting considerable time into revising for it.

This chapter is about how to revise a novel.

This was a tricky one… reread the novel or go out on the town?

What the examiners are looking for

✓ Do you know the novel well?

✓ Do you understand how the writer has used language to create effects, and can you refer to particular examples?

✓ Can you say what you think the novel means or is about?

✓ Can you show your understanding of the characters?

✓ Can you express your personal response to the novel? This means showing that you have thought about it, and that you have ideas and reactions of your own; it might mean writing what you liked or disliked about it, too.

✓ Can you show some awareness of the social, cultural and historical context in which the novel is written or set?

Tackling the exam paper

Reading the paper

Find the two questions that relate to the novel that you have studied. It is very important that you read both questions before you choose one to answer. Think about what you know and don't dismiss a question too quickly. A question may look hard, but it may actually encourage you to think and write in interesting ways. If you think carefully, you may have a lot to write about it.

In *Chapter 9* (page 109) there are examples of questions, with advice on how to read them.

Planning

Quickly organise your ideas before starting to write. You could make a list of points or a diagram of your ideas: never just begin writing. (See the section on *Practising planning and writing* on page 66.)

*He now regretted jumping
in with both feet…*

Referring to the text

You will, of course, have to look back at the text to help you to
plan your answer, to find ideas and examples to refer to, and to
choose words and phrases to quote. You will not have time to read
pages word for word, and so you will need to be good at skimming
and scanning. The section called *How to practise skimming and
scanning the text* (page 63) will help you to do this.

Checking and correcting

Leave yourself time to check your answers at the end. Five minutes
should be enough. For example:

Look for missing punctuation

Check that you
have set out
quotations correctly

Make corrections neatly

Beginning your revision

Reread the novel. It really is worth leaving time for yourself to do this.

Remind yourself of the order of events in the novel. It might help to write a flow diagram, showing what happens, and which characters are involved.

Piggy and Ralph on beach
↓
Finding of conch
↓
Gathering of b
↓
Jack and
Expl
Pig

Look back over all the notes that you have made or been given when you studied the novel, and make sure that you understand them. You need to know about the characters, and about the main ideas in the novel.

Annotating the text (2004 exam only)

It is very important that you do not spend too long in the exam looking for references in the book: know where they are! Mark key passages with a line in the margin. Underline useful quotations, or mark them in the margin so that you can find them easily. Concentrate on material to do with the main character(s) and with the main ideas or aspects of the novel that you have looked at. The process of doing this annotation is very good revision in itself.

Don't forget the rules about annotation: you are not allowed to write more than one or two words at a time in the margin. Your teacher will be able to tell you whether you have annotated too much.

Make sure that you use a pencil, not a pen, unless it is your own copy of the novel.

 ## How to practise skimming and scanning the text

This is an essential skill for this part of the exam, so that you do not spend ages looking for quotations or examples to refer to.

Remember, this kind of reading is not about reading individual words, one after the other. It is about looking at large pieces of text, and quickly finding particular words or ideas in them. You should get used to looking at a whole page at a time. Try moving your eye quickly down the page, resting at three or four points, and looking for key words or phrases.

Most of the revision activities suggested later in this chapter involve this sort of searching in the text, but you could try this as well.

- Pick a character. Skim through one chapter looking for all the references to that character.
- Pick a theme. Skim through another chapter looking for the parts which relate to this theme.
- Skim through the whole novel, picking out any events, dialogue or descriptions that you think are important.

 ## Social, historical and cultural context

One of the things that the examiners will be looking for is evidence that you are aware of the time and place in which the novel was written, and about what mattered to people then or there.

If the novel was written some time ago:
- how does it reflect the way people thought at the time, or what they valued?
- how does it relate to the history of the time?
- how does the way it is written, or the ideas in it, reflect the country or culture it is from?

You will have discussed this when you studied the novel, and it is worth reminding yourself about it now.

You should not write about this at length in the exam, but do try to show that you are aware of it, even if that only means writing a brief paragraph or two. The examiners will not be impressed by pages of background information – they want you to show what you know about the text.

Quoting

It is essential that you quote from the text to support the points that you make in the essay. Well-chosen quotations show your knowledge of the text. They also show that you understand the point that you are making.

Quotations should be brief and should not dominate the essay. As a rough guide, they should not take up any more than about 15% of the essay. Never quote more than two or three lines. Usually, this will be too much. The kind of quotation that shows that you really know the text well is when you weave quoted words into your own sentences. For example:

> From his first appearance, Jack is associated with death and evil. His "tall, thin and bony" body is skeletal – an image of death – and his "floating cloak" is reminiscent of a vampire – a personification of evil. His red hair is traditionally (and stereotypically) associated with impulsiveness and aggression, and his eyes are "ready to turn, to anger". (The "black cap", with its association with judges condemning prisoners to death, takes on a grim significance as the story unfolds.)

Practising planning and writing

One of the most important ways to revise for this part of the exam is to get used to tackling the kinds of questions that are in the paper. Ask your teacher for examples of these to practise with. Look at the advice on *Practising planning and writing* in *Chapter 1*.

Title underlined   Brief introductory paragraph

4.   <u>Lord of the Flies</u> ends with the destruction of the boys' society on the island. Yet Ralph seems to weep for more than this: "the end of innocence, the darkness of man's heart."

I believe that Golding, writing shortly after the end of the Second World War, wanted to show that

Reference to the question; also quotation (see page 119)

Personal response

Social, historical and cultural context

Other ways to revise a novel

*Jenny was up in her room trying
out some novel revision…*

The following suggestions for revision activities are graded as easy,
less easy and hard.

 Easy

 Make a list of the characters in the novel and write down a few
words about each. You could also make a diagram showing how
the characters relate to each other.

• • • • •

Imagine that a publisher has asked you to write a short
description for the back of a new edition of the novel. It must be
no more than 100 words long, and it must tell a reader what the
novel is about without giving away the whole story. It must also
give an idea of what kind of story it is, some information about
the people in it, and why a reader might enjoy it. Try to sum up
for the reader what important ideas they will find in the novel.

• • • • •

Choose an important event in the novel. Imagine that you are one of the characters involved, and write between 60 and 70 words about what happened. To help you to get the most from your writing, think about these questions:

- Why was it important?
- How were you involved?
- How did you feel about what happened?

• • • • •

 Pick one character and try to write for five minutes about that character:

- What can you remember about them?
- What do they do in the story?
- Why are they important?

Then try this with other characters.

• • • • •

Choose a theme or idea that you talked about when you read the book in class.

Write down at least three places in the novel where this idea is important. For each place, write down which characters are involved, and how what they say and do makes the idea clear.

Then find one key quotation from each place in the novel that you might use if you are writing about this idea in the exam. Try it for several ideas and give yourself just a few minutes for each.

Less easy

 Choose a main character.

On a piece of paper, do a brainstorm around the character. You should include important scenes that they are involved in and themes or ideas in the novel that they represent. Note at least five quotations which you might use in an exam if you were writing about this character. Write down how this character changes during the novel. If you find this helpful, do it for more characters.

• • • • •

 Choose a theme or main idea in the novel. For example, it might be how people use the power they have, how people are changed by their experiences, or how they behave under pressure.

On a piece of paper, do a brainstorm around this idea. You should include scenes in which the idea is important, characters who show something about this idea, and at least five quotations which you might use in an exam if you were writing about it.

If you find this helpful, do it for more ideas.

• • • • •

Choose an aspect of the writer's technique in the novel. For example, it might be the use of symbols, allegory, descriptions of places and characters, or a particular narrative voice.

On a piece of paper, do a brainstorm around this technique. You should include scenes in which this technique is clear, and at least five quotations which you might use in an exam if you were writing about it. Next to each quotation, explain why you chose it to illustrate the writer's technique.

If you find this helpful, do it for other aspects of the writer's technique.

If the chapters in your novel have headings, choose four or five of them. Make notes on how each heading relates to the themes and events in the chapter in particular, and in the novel in general. This will give you a useful summary of key points, and a helpful revision aid.

If you find this helpful, do it for every chapter.

• • • • •

 Imagine you are one of the characters in the novel. Write as though you are reflecting on the events of the whole story. Looking back, what do you remember most clearly? How do you feel now about what happened? What have you learned – about yourself, about other characters, or about the world?

This will help you to revise the significance of your chosen character, and to explore events and ideas from an alternative perspective.

If you find this helpful, do it for more characters.

Some questions were harder than others…

Hard

The first three activities are similar to the 'less easy' ones, but encourage you to explore more deeply on your own.

 Choose who you consider to be the main characters. For each one, make notes on the following things:

- How they relate to other characters.
- What you learn about them from this.

Look for three or four key quotations or examples to refer to in an exam. Does the character represent an idea or theme? Do they help you to understand an idea or theme in the novel?

Write down some key moments in the novel where this becomes clear, and then look for short quotations for each that you could use in an exam.

• • • • •

 Choose what you consider to be the main themes or ideas in the novel. They might include, for example, human nature, power relationships, racial tensions, conflict, history or the way that circumstances change behaviour.

Make notes on each idea. How is the idea developed through the novel? Pick out some key events which you would refer to if you were writing about this idea, and write down at least one short quotation from each. Are there particular characters who represent or illuminate the idea? How?

• • • • •

 Choose what you consider to be the most important features of the writer's technique in the novel. For example, the use of symbolism, allegory, description of places and characters, a particular narrative voice, structural devices, or the use of particular kinds of language.

Write about where in the novel these features of technique are particularly significant, and consider how and why. Select appropriate quotations to support your points.

• • • • •

 Imagine that you are the writer of the novel that you have studied. You have just finished writing it and you want it to be published. Write a letter to send to publishers, persuading them that your novel is a good investment for them.

You will need to explain:
- what kind of novel it is
- what kind of audience it is written for
- what the main themes are
- main features of the plot
- techniques you have used in writing the novel
- why it will appeal to the target audience.

Make sure that the letter is long enough to communicate your main points, but brief enough to be interesting.

This is an excellent way of consolidating your knowledge of the novel, and helps you to become used to writing about it as a whole.

• • • • •

Do some research on the writer of your novel. You might be able to find articles or books about him or her in a library or on the Internet, which will give you new ideas or perspectives on the novel.

7 Revising short stories

In **Section A** of the **English Literature Paper**, you will have to write for 45 minutes either about a novel or about the short stories from the AQA Anthology you have studied. Remember that this one essay counts for 30% of the total English Literature mark, which is as much as all your English Literature coursework put together, so it is worth putting considerable time into revising for it.

This chapter is about how to revise the short stories.

"Enough of the TALL stories... now where's your SHORT story?"

What the examiners are looking for

✓ Do you know the short stories well?

✓ Do you understand how the writers have used language to create effects, and can you refer to particular examples?

✓ Can you say what you think the stories mean or are about?

✓ Can you show your understanding of the characters?

✓ Can you express your personal response to the stories? This means showing that you have thought about them, and that you have ideas and reactions of your own; it might mean writing what you liked or disliked about them, too.

✓ Can you show some awareness of the social, cultural and historical context in which each story is written or set?

✓ Can you compare stories? This will usually mean comparing two stories.

✓ Are you aware of what short stories are – their forms and features, and how writers use them to create particular effects?

AaHa!

Comparing the stories

One of the main things that the examiners are looking for in this section of the exam is the ability to compare the stories. You will be writing about two or three stories, and you must show that you are aware of how they are similar – in the way they are written and in what they are saying – and how they are different. For example:

	Snowdrops	Growing up
How the characters change and what they learn	• loss of innocence (disillusionment – frailty of snowdrops represents reality of adult world)	• loss of innocence (girls rejecting their childish relationship with father)
How the characters are treated by grown-ups	• boy kept from truth • protected	• father trying to hold on to his connection with the children • father confused about how to treat his daughters
Methods the writers use to show characters' thoughts and feelings	• child's viewpoint • childish language; simple sentences and narrative • symbolism (bacon, snowdrops) • twist at end	• adult's viewpoint • references to the past • frightening descriptions of girls' violence • symbolism (garden; dirt)

The following words and phrases are useful for starting or joining sentences, when you are comparing texts:

Although...
In the first text...
Compared with...
While one text...

...in the other...
However,...
Nevertheless,...
...the second text...
On the other hand,...
In comparison,...
Meanwhile,...
In contrast,...
...whereas...
...while...
Similarly,...
Equally,...
In the same way...

Tackling the exam paper

Reading the paper

Find the questions that relate to your short stories. It is very important that you read all three questions before you choose one to answer. Think about what you know and don't dismiss a question too quickly. A question may look hard, but it may actually get you thinking in interesting ways. If you think carefully, you may have a lot to write about it.

Chapter 9 (page 109) provides examples of questions, with advice.

Planning

The examiners will be looking for evidence that you have ordered your ideas before starting to write. Make a quick list of points or a diagram of your ideas: don't just launch into the writing. (See *Practising planning and writing*, page 82.)

Referring to the text

You will, of course, have to look back at the stories before and as you write your answers:

* to help you to plan your answer
* to find ideas and examples to refer to
* to choose words and phrases to quote.

You will not have time to read pages word for word, and so you will need to be good at skimming and scanning. The section *How to practise skimming and scanning the text* (page 79) will help you to do this.

Checking and correcting

Leave yourself time to check your answers at the end. Five minutes should be enough. For example:

Look for missing punctuation

Check that you have set out quotations correctly

of the stories

There are example of t
symbolism, and other device
"crowned. The repeated refe
power. The story is also
rabbits.
                    story
    Later in the play there o
images of evil, despair, a
reader feeling that this wa

Make corrections neatly

Beginning your revision

Reread the stories that you have studied. It is essential that you leave time to do this.

Remind yourself of the order of events in each story. It might help to write a flow diagram, showing what happens, and the characters involved.

'Growing Up'

Quick returns home
children not ther
↓
Girls in garden ign
attack dog
↓
Girls turn
attack

Look back over all the notes that you have made or been given when you studied the stories, and make sure that you understand them.

You need to know about the characters and the main ideas in each story. To help with this, you should make a list of the characters in each story, and write down a few words about them. You could also make a diagram showing how the characters in each story relate to each other.

It is essential that you know how the stories can be compared and connected with each other. For most of the revision activities on pages 83 to 86 you need to choose two or three of the stories to work with. This is something that you will have worked on in class.

Annotating the text (2004 exam only)

It is important that you do not spend too much time in the exam looking for references in the Anthology: know where they are! Mark key passages with a line in the margin. Underline useful quotations, or mark them in the margin so that you can find them easily. Concentrate on material to do with the main character(s), and with the main ideas or aspects of the stories that you have looked at. The process of doing this annotation is very good revision in itself.

Don't forget the rules about annotation: you are not allowed to write more than one or two words at a time in the margin. Your teacher will be able to tell you whether you have annotated too much.

How to practise skimming and scanning the text

Skimming and scanning are essential skills for this part of the exam. Use them so that you do not spend too long looking for quotations or examples to refer to.

Remember, this kind of reading is not about reading individual words, one after the other. It is about looking at large pieces of text, and quickly finding particular words or ideas in them. You need to get used to looking at a whole page at a time. Try moving your eye quickly down the page, resting at three or four points, and looking for key words or phrases.

Most of the revision activities suggested in this chapter involve this sort of searching in the text, but you could try the one below as well.

- Take a story. Skim through it looking for all the references to a particular theme or idea.
- Then practise looking for moments in each story that you can remember and which might be useful. They might include a piece of dialogue, a description of a place or a person, or a significant event.
- Skim through each story, picking out any events, dialogue or descriptions that you think are important.

Social, historical and cultural context

It is important that you have some knowledge about the times and places in which your stories were written, and about what mattered to people then. You will have discussed this when you studied the stories, and it is worth reminding yourself about it now. You might also want to find out more about it.

If the story was written some time ago:
- how does it reflect the way people thought at the time, or what they valued?
- how does it relate to the history of the time?
- how does the way it is written, or the ideas in it, reflect the country or culture it is from?

You should not write about this at length in the exam, but you should try to show that you are aware of it, which probably means writing only a short paragraph or two. The examiners will not be impressed by pages of background information – they want you to show what you know about the stories.

Quoting

When you are writing about the stories in the exam, it is important that you quote from the texts to support the points that you make in the essay. Well-chosen quotations show your knowledge of the texts. They also show that you understand the points that you are making.

Quotations should be brief and should not dominate the essay. As a rough guide, they should not take up any more than about 15% of the essay. Never quote more than two or three lines.

Usually, this will be too much. The kind of quotation that shows that you really know the text well is when you weave quoted words into your own sentences. For example:

> The writer describes the snowdrops in language which reflects the boy's "slow sad disappointment". The flowers are "simple" and will not "turn marvellous in front of his eyes." The parts of the flowers are "minute", "little", and "miniature"; they have "greyish leaves".

Each word or phrase is a separate quotation, and so needs its own quotation marks

Practising planning and writing

One of the most important ways to revise for this part of the exam is to get used to tackling the kinds of questions that are in the paper. Ask your teacher for examples of these to work on. Look at the advice on *Practising planning and writing* in *Chapter 1*. There is an example plan on page 75.

The questions will usually ask you to compare stories

A quotation is one way to start your essay which will engage the reader

"She's growing up – and so am I."

In both 'Snowdrops' and 'Growing Up' adults and children learn and change. (However,) while one writer presents the child's viewpoint, the other explores the adult's.

From the opening of 'Snowdrops', the childish language conveys the innocence of the boy and his view of the world. ("...the schoolkeeper's house, where they weren't allowed to go"). At the start of 'Growing Up', Robert Quick thinks of his daughters as "small girls" – language which reflects his inability to see how they are growing.

Short introduction to the main point(s) of the essay

It is effective to compare the stories as you go along

Always quote or refer to details, to support your ideas

Write about how the writers use language to convey ideas

Other ways to revise the stories

The following suggestions for revision activities are graded as easy, less easy and hard.

 Easy

 Choose a main character from one of the stories. Write down how this character changes during the story, or what the character learns. Write down at least three quotations that you could use if you were writing about the character in the exam.

Then do this for the main characters from at least two other stories. The ways in which characters develop or learn is often an important idea in short stories.

•　•　•　•　•

 Choose an important event in one of the stories. Imagine that you are one of the characters involved, and write between 60 and 70 words about what happened. To help you to get the most from your writing, think about these questions:
• Why was it important?
• How were you involved?
• How did you feel about what happened?

If you find this useful, do the same for one or two of the other stories.

•　•　•　•　•

 Choose a theme or idea that can be found in more than one story. Find one key quotation from each story that you might use if you are writing about this idea in the exam. This will give you confidence that you do have things to write.

Try it for two or three other ideas, and give yourself just a few minutes for each.

•　•　•　•　•

Imagine that you have been asked to choose two stories to be read aloud on the radio. They should be connected in some way. Write a short introduction (about 100 words) to be read out before the stories, explaining to the listeners why the stories fit together. Be careful not to give away the endings.

 Less easy

 Imagine you are a character in one of the stories. Write as though you are reflecting on the events of the whole story. Looking back, what do you remember most clearly? How do you feel now about what happened? What have you learned – about yourself, about other characters, or about the world?

This will help you to revise the significance of your chosen character, and to explore events and ideas from an alternative perspective. If you find this helpful, do it for characters from other stories.

• • • • •

 Look at the titles of the stories. For each one, write some notes on how the title relates to the themes and events in the story. This should help you to think about what is important in the story.

• • • • •

 Choose two stories which seem to be connected in some way. Use the list of connecting words and phrases on page 75 to practise writing sentences which compare the two stories – how they are similar and how they are different.

 • • • • •

 Choose one story and think about a technique that the writer has used. For example, it might be the use of symbols, allegory, descriptions of places and characters, or a particular narrative voice.

Write down at least five quotations which you might use in an exam if you were writing about it. Next to each quotation, explain why you chose it to illustrate the writer's technique.

You could try doing this for other techniques in the same story, or for other stories.

• • • • •

Look at the ending of each story that you are revising, and think about the following things:

- How did you feel when you got to the end of the story? Why?
- Was the ending what you had been led to expect, or was it different?
- How did the writer lead up to the ending?
- What do you think the writer wanted you to think or feel at the end?

Make some notes on these ideas. You could then choose two stories. Write about 150 words, comparing the two endings.

 Hard

Choose two characters, from different stories, who can be compared in some way. Make notes on the following things:

- How do they relate to other characters?
- What do you learn about them from this?
- Does each character represent an idea or theme?
- Do they help you to understand an idea or theme in the story?

Write down some key moments in the story where this becomes clear, and then look for short quotations for each that you could use in an exam. How does each character change or develop in the story? What do you think connects the characters?

• • • • •

Choose a theme or idea which can be found in more than one story. For example, it might be human nature, appearance and reality, power relationships, tensions between generations, history or the way that circumstances change behaviour.

How is the idea developed in each story? Are there particular characters who represent or illuminate the idea? How? What similarities or differences are there in the way that the stories treat the idea?

• • • • •

 In one story, choose what you consider to be the most important features of the writer's technique. For example, the use of symbolism, allegory, description of places and characters, a particular narrative voice, structural devices, or the use of particular kinds of language.

Note how the writer has used these techniques and why. Select appropriate quotations to support your points.

• • • • •

 Imagine that you are a film maker. You are asked to choose two of the Anthology stories to film for television. The stories should have themes, ideas or situations in common. Write a letter explaining why the stories you have chosen would work well together and why they would be suitable for filming.

This will help you to think about connections between stories. Considering how the stories might be filmed is a very good way of thinking about their structures, their moods and what is most important in them.

8 Words to revise

When you are writing about a text – whether it is a poem, a novel, a short story, a newspaper article, a leaflet or any other piece of writing – there are special, technical words that you may need to use. Here is a checklist of some of them:

- ☐ Accent
- ☐ Adjective
- ☐ Adverb
- ☐ Allegory
- ☐ Alliteration
- ☐ Ambiguity
- ☐ Anchor
- ☐ Anthropomorphism
- ☐ Archaic
- ☐ Assertion
- ☐ Assonance
- ☐ Audience
- ☐ Banner
- ☐ Bathos
- ☐ Broadsheet
- ☐ Bullet points
- ☐ Button
- ☐ Caption
- ☐ Colloquialism
- ☐ Couplet
- ☐ Cropping
- ☐ Cross-heads
- ☐ Dialect
- ☐ Diction

"There are all SORTS of words in here...," he shrieked

- ☐ Emotive language
- ☐ Fable
- ☐ Fact
- ☐ Foot
- ☐ Frame
- ☐ Genre
- ☐ Headline
- ☐ Hypertext
- ☐ Iambic pentameter
- ☐ Icon
- ☐ Imagery
- ☐ Imperative
- ☐ Layout
- ☐ Logo
- ☐ Masthead
- ☐ Metaphor
- ☐ Metre
- ☐ Microcosm
- ☐ Mise-en-scène
- ☐ Mood
- ☐ Myth
- ☐ Narrative
- ☐ Narrator
- ☐ Noun
- ☐ Octave
- ☐ Onomatopoeia
- ☐ Opinion (implicit and explicit)
- ☐ Pace
- ☐ Parody
- ☐ Patois
- ☐ Personification
- ☐ Persuasive language
- ☐ Phonetic spelling
- ☐ Plot
- ☐ Point of view/viewpoint
- ☐ Pronoun
- ☐ Puns
- ☐ Reading path
- ☐ Received pronunciation (RP)
- ☐ Register
- ☐ Representation
- ☐ Rhetorical question
- ☐ Rhythm
- ☐ Satire
- ☐ Sestet
- ☐ Sibilance
- ☐ Simile
- ☐ Slang
- ☐ Sonnet
- ☐ Standard English
- ☐ Stanza
- ☐ Stereotype
- ☐ Structure
- ☐ Syllable
- ☐ Symbol
- ☐ Tabloid
- ☐ Text
- ☐ Theme
- ☐ Tone
- ☐ Trochaic tetrameter
- ☐ Verb
- ☐ Voice

Below is a list of words or phrases that you might need to revise, with brief reminders of what they mean.

Accent

This is the way that people from particular places pronounce words.

Accent is often important to people's sense of identity, and there is still a lot of prejudice about accents. Look at how writers sometimes imitate accent in the way they write words down. What effect do you think this is meant to have? (See **Phonetic spelling** *and* **Received pronunciation**.*)*

Adjective

An adjective is a word which describes a **noun**.

For example, "cold", "clever", "happy", "exciting"... .

Adverb

An adverb is a word which describes how something is done, and is usually put next to a **verb**.

For example, "quickly", "happily", "predictably", "softly"... .

Allegory

An allegory is a story which can be read on more than one level. The characters and events in an allegory always represent something more general than just themselves.

For example, the novel Lord of the Flies, *by William Golding, can be read just as a story about a group of boys on an island, or it can also be seen as a description of how people come into conflict with each other in the wider world. The animals in* Animal Farm, *by George Orwell, represent particular people in the political history of the Soviet Union. (See* **Fable**.*)*

Alliteration

This is where words close to each other begin with the same letter. You will find it used quite often in newspaper **headlines**, in poetry, or in song lyrics.

When you find examples of alliteration, always think about its effects. Does it make the language more striking and easier to remember? ("Brown's Budget Beats Blues") Does it emphasise the rhythm of the words? ("Full fathom five thy father lies") Does it work like **onomatopoeia**, *imitating the sound of what it describes?* *("Sudden successive flights of bullets streak the silence")*

Ambiguity

If something is ambiguous, then it could mean more than one thing, such as the newspaper **headline** "Giant Waves Down Tunnel".

It might be possible to interpret a line or a word in a poem in more than one way. Sometimes this is deliberate. For example, "generous laughter" could mean that the laughter is kind and giving, or that it there is lots of it. Sexual double-entendre is an example of deliberate ambiguity. For example, in The Duchess of Malfi, *by John Webster, an intruder in the Duchess's bed chamber is described as having "a pistol in his great cod-piece".*

Anchor

The way we read a text can be anchored, or tied down. For example, a **caption** might 'tell' the reader to read a photograph in a newspaper in a particular way.

A picture of students sitting in rows, taking an exam, will be interpreted very differently with the caption "Captive candidates" than with the caption "Lined up for success". (See **Caption***.)*

Anthropomorphism

This is when animals or objects are given human qualities or abilities, such as when animals in cartoons or children's stories talk, wear clothes, and behave like people.

In Animal Farm, *all of the animals are given human characteristics. They are able to speak, reason and organise themselves as humans do. Think about why writers use this device. What does it allow them to do? Look for examples of anthropomorphism in everyday life, in the way that people talk about animals, cars, belongings and so on.*
(See **Personification***.)*

Archaic

If language is archaic, then it is old-fashioned or not in use any more. For example, the word "perambulator" has been replaced by "pram".

Sometimes, modern writers use archaic language to create a particular association or feeling. How is the effect of the word "wireless" different from "radio"? To a modern reader, the language of older texts will often seem archaic:

> "Thou tricksy Puck!
> With antic toys so funnily bestuck"

Assertion

This is a statement which is not backed up with **facts** or information.

For example, the statement "GCSE exams are obviously becoming easier" is an example of assertion. It is stated as though it must be true, and does not allow the reader to disagree. Look for examples in persuasive texts, and think about why they are there. (See **Opinion**.)

Assonance

Assonance is where words close to each other contain the same vowel sounds: "With dying light the silent fall of night".

Does it make the language easier to remember? Does it help to create a **mood** or feeling through the repeated sounds? Does it work like **onomatopoeia**, imitating the sound of what it describes?

Audience

The audience is the people who read a text or listen to what is being said. The people who buy a particular newspaper, for example.

When you are talking or writing about a text, think about the audience that it is intended for: Who are they? How is the form and language suitable for this audience? What does the writer assume about the audience? What does the text demand from the audience?

When you are writing or speaking, you have to keep your audience in mind. Is the language and form that you have chosen appropriate? How do you want your audience to think, feel or react?

Banner

On a Web page, a banner is an advertisement which links to another Web page. It is often in the shape of a long rectangle across the top or bottom of the page.

Bathos

When a writer appears to be building up to something, then deliberately ends in an anticlimax, he/she is using bathos. This is almost always comic:

"Punark the Sorcerer was held in awe throughout the dark lands for his terrible powers of destruction, his unrivalled mastery of the ways of magic, his ferocious hatred for humankind, and his excellent recipe for lasagne."

Broadsheet

Broadsheet newspapers, such as *The Times* and *The Independent*, usually present the news in detail, and have sections which comment on and analyse news events. (See **Tabloid**.)

Bullet points

- These are bullet points.
- *They are used to make ideas clearer on the page, by separating them out, with a dot at the start of each one.*
- *Look at how they are used in informative and persuasive texts, where the ideas have to be as clear as possible.*

Button

In an electronic document (such as a page on a Web site or CD-ROM), a button is a graphic which can be clicked with the mouse, to make something happen or to link to another page.

Caption

A caption is a short piece of text which goes with a picture. It guides the way we read the image.

*For example, in a newspaper, most photographs have a caption underneath them. Think about how the caption is meant to affect your reading of the image. (See **Anchor**.)*

Colloquialism

A colloquial expression is one that people use in everyday speech, but not in more formal writing.

For example, "bloke" is a colloquial word for "man", and "getting stuck in" is a colloquial phrase for "starting". Look at how writers use colloquialisms to create an informal mood, or to give a natural **voice** *to a poem, for example. (See* **Register** *and* **Slang**.*)*

Couplet

This is a pair of rhyming lines in a poem, such as the last two lines of Shakespeare's 18th Sonnet:

"So long as men can breathe or eyes can see,
So long lives this, and this gives life to thee."

Think about the particular effect of rhyming couplets, especially at the ends of poems or **stanzas**.

Cropping

If parts of a picture are cut off at the edges, this is called cropping. In media texts, look at the edges of images.

Cross-heads

In a newspaper, magazine, or leaflet, cross-heads are words or phrases extracted from the text and placed between paragraphs. They are most common in **tabloid** newspapers.

Notice how cross-heads are chosen to keep the reader's interest, or to guide the way the story is meant to be read. (See **Anchor**.*)*

Dialect

People from different places or cultures often have different versions of the same language – with some different words, different expressions, and different ways of constructing sentences.

For example, in Yorkshire dialect, "frame thissen" means "get yourself organised". In Scotland, you might hear the sentence "That door is needing locked", which shows different sentence structure from Standard English.

Oral poetry (poetry which is passed on by word of mouth) will often be in dialect. For example, the ballad 'The Twa Corbies' is in Scots dialect, reflecting the speech of the place where it originated, as shown on the following page:

> *"As I was walking all alane*
> *I heard twa corbies making a mane"*

You should look for examples of how writers have used dialect forms and think about why they have done this.

(This is not the same as **Accent***. See* **Standard English** *and* **Phonetic spelling***.)*

Diction

In a text, diction refers to the kind of words a writer has chosen.

It can be useful to think about this if you are talking or writing about a text. You might write about how a writer has chosen a lot of **colloquial** *words, or technical words, or words relating to nature, for example. If you wanted to say that there was a lot of old-fashioned language in a text, you might refer to the "archaic diction".*

Emotive language

This is language which is used to make a reader or listener feel a particular emotion.

Always think about the effects of emotive language. What emotions does the writer want to make the reader feel, and why? It is used a lot in persuasive texts, such as advertisements, but also look for it in places where you might not expect it: in newspaper reports, for example. How does the headline "Jail This Beast Now" above a report of a murder trial suggest the reader should feel? (See **Persuasive language***.)*

Fable

A fable is a story with a moral message.

Traditionally, fables have often been stories about animals, written or told to teach children about how to behave towards others, such as Aesop's Fables. The novel Animal Farm *is a complicated fable written for adults, with a warning about the dangers of power. (See* **Allegory***.)*

Fact

A fact is something that can be proved to be true.

Foot

See **Metre**.

Frame

In an electronic document (such as a page on a Web site or CD-ROM), a frame is like a page within the page – a box in which text or pictures can appear and be changed.

Genre

A genre is a "type" or "kind" of text. (In French, "genre" means "type".)

For example, in stories and films there are genres such as science fiction, horror, war, romance, comedy, and so on. Newspaper reports, magazine articles, leaflets and advertisements are all examples of non-literary genres.

It is important to think about what texts in a particular genre have in common. The features that they share are called the conventions of the genre. These conventions might include particular types of language, **layout***, or content. In a story or film, they might include typical settings, characters, events,* **themes***, or ways that a story can develop.*

Headline

This is the heading for a newspaper article.

Think about what effects it is meant to have on the reader.

Hypertext

In an electronic document (such as a page on a Web site or CD-ROM), hypertext is a word or phrase which, when clicked with the mouse pointer, links to another part of the document, or to a another Web site.

Iambic pentameter

See **Metre**.

Icon

An icon is a kind of **symbol**. A graphic icon is a small picture.

You will find examples in leaflets, on computer screens and Web pages, in magazines and other texts. They make it easy for a reader to find their way quickly around a text.

Imagery

Writers or speakers often create "pictures" which help the reader or listener to imagine something clearly.

For example, "as flat as a millpond" is an image to describe unusually calm waters. **Metaphor, personification** *and* **simile** *are types of imagery. Which of these does Wilfred Owen use in the following line from 'Exposure'?*

"the merciless iced east winds that knive us..."
(See **Metaphor, Personification** *and* **Simile***.)*

Imperative

An imperative **verb** is one which tells the reader or listener to do something, like an instruction.

"Buy now!", "Stay there!" and "Think about it!" are examples of imperatives. Look for how these are used in persuasive texts.

Layout

This is the way that words, pictures, graphics, paragraphs, lines of text, headings, subheadings and **symbols** are arranged on the page.

This can affect the way something is read, and the effect it has. Look at this especially when you are writing about and comparing leaflets, articles or other informative and persuasive texts.

Logo

This is a design which symbolises an organisation or company. You may find logos on advertisements or leaflets.

"Actually it says 'logo'..."

Masthead

On the front page of a newspaper, the masthead is the name of the paper, printed at the top of the page. Think about how the design of the masthead (font, colour, size) tells the reader about the newspaper and its approach to the news.

Metaphor

This is when something is described by saying it is something else.

"What are you like...?"

*When you are talking or writing about a metaphor, always think about its effect. For example, "A monster chewing at the beach" is a way of describing the frightening power and animal-like energy of the sea. Think about the effect you can create with metaphors in your own writing, too. Look for examples of metaphors in everyday speech. Remember that a metaphor is different from a **simile**, because it says that something actually is something else, not that it is like something else. An extended metaphor is where one metaphor leads on to others. For example, in the opening of* Hard Times, *by Charles Dickens, Mr Gradgrind's forehead is described as a "wall". It then makes sense to describe his head as a "warehouse" and his eyes as "cellarage".*

Metre

In poetry, the **syllables** in each line are sometimes stressed in a regular pattern. This is called metre.

To show this pattern, it can be useful to mark where the stresses fall, with slashes for stressed syllables, and circles for unstressed ones, like this:

o / o / o / o / o /

"He threw the snowball hard and hit his friend,

$$o \quad / \quad o \quad / \quad o \quad / \quad o \quad / \quad o \quad /$$

He did not know, or think, how fun might end."

*Read this out loud a couple of times and listen to how the stresses in the lines emphasise particular words. Look for metre in poems, and look for how the **rhythm** can help to create a tone – cheery, or insistent, perhaps. Look for places where the rhythm suddenly changes: what is the effect?*

*Each pair of stressed and unstressed syllables is called a **foot**. An unstressed syllable followed by a stressed syllable (o /) is called an iamb. A stressed syllable followed by an unstressed syllable (/ o) is called a trochee. Different lengths of lines have different technical names. A line with five feet is called pentameter, one with four feet is called tetrameter, a line with three feet is called trimeter.*

Two common types of metre, particularly in Shakespeare's verse, are iambic pentameter and trochaic tetrameter.

- **Iambic pentameter** *has five iambic feet in each line, like the example above.*

- **Trochaic tetrameter** *has four trochaic feet in each line, like this:*

$$/ \quad o \quad / \quad o \quad \quad / \quad o \quad / \quad o$$
"If we shadows have offended,

$$/ \quad \quad o \quad / \quad o \quad \quad / \quad o \quad / \quad o$$
Think but this, and all is mended"

*(See **Sonnet** and **Syllable**.)*

Microcosm

In a story, a microcosm is a miniature version of the world.

For example, you might describe a school as a microcosm of society, with its own rules, leaders, ways of doing things, and so on. In the novel, Lord of the Flies, *the island is a microcosm for the whole world: all the events and characters on the island represent aspects of the world as a whole.*

Mise-en-scène

In a photograph, mise-en-scène means everything included in the image. (In French, it means 'placed in the picture').

*Think about what has been included in a picture. How has it been chosen to create particular effects, and what are these effects? (See **Cropping**.)*

Mood

This is the atmosphere or the feeling that a piece of writing creates.

A poem might have an ominous, sinister mood, or it might have a restless, yearning mood, for example. Look at how writers use language to create particular moods.

Myth

This is a story originally told to explain something, or to represent important truths.

For example, the story of the Garden of Eden can be read as the story of how all people are tempted into sin, and lose innocence.

Narrative

Narrative is the way a story is told in any text.
(See **Narrator** and **Structure**.)

Narrator

The narrator is the person telling a story.

A first person narrative is where the narrator describes their own experience: "I walked into the room...". The narrator is then a part of the story, and might tell the reader what he or she is thinking and feeling. A third person narrative is where the narrator describes what other people do. "She walked into the room...". The narrator can be outside the story, and can be distanced from what is happening.

Noun

A noun is a word which names something.

This might be a person, place, object, feeling, or idea. For example, "Paula", "London", "pen", "happiness", "education"...

Octave

See **Sonnet**.

Onomatopoeia

An onomatopoeic word is one which sounds like what it describes.

"Crash", "whisper", "rustle", "squelch", "bleat" and "snip" are examples of onomatopoeic words.

These are used by writers to create atmosphere, or to make an experience

…what with all the distractions of the exam room he had forgotten what 'onomatopoeia' meant…

seem real. Think about how you can use onomatopoeia in your own writing, too. And know how to spell it.

Opinion (implicit and explicit)

An opinion is something that one person believes, but which somebody else might not believe.

Explicit opinion is where somebody states their own view directly. For example, "I think young people are rude" is an explicit opinion. Implicit opinion is where the view is not stated directly, but it comes across anyway. For example, in "The young person was typically rude" the speaker's opinion of young people is implied by the word "typically". Look for these in persuasive texts, and make sure that you can tell the difference between **facts** *and opinions. (See* **Fact**.)

Pace

A piece of writing can seem to move quickly or slowly as it is read. This is known as its pace.

Look at how the pace of the following two examples is created by:

- *long or short sentences and words*
- *repetition*
- *punctuation*
- **mood**
- **alliteration**
- *long or short vowel sounds.*

"Stretching lazily in the sunshine, listening to the soft, slow sounds of summer lingering on the heavy air, she drifted languidly into sleep."

"Now. I have to move now. Quick! Quick! He's almost caught me! Running, almost tripping on the broken ground. Sharp stones underfoot. Can't breathe, can't see! Where can I hide?"

Parody

If you parody a text, you make fun of it by imitating it and exaggerating its features.

Patois

A patois is a spoken **dialect** of English which is very different from spoken **Standard English**.

When it is written down (for example in a poem or a story) this is usually to create the effect of people speaking in their own voice. John Agard's poem 'Half Caste' is written in the patois of Guyana, where he was born.

Personification

This is where something inanimate (not alive) is written or spoken about as though it were alive.

For example, in Wilfred Owen's poem 'Exposure', the weather is treated as a living enemy: "Dawn masses in the east her melancholy army."

"Okay... stop writing"

Sometimes an idea or a quality is turned into a character. For example, you might decide that a character in a story is a "personification of goodness", or a "personification of bravery". In pictures, Death is traditionally personified as a hooded figure with a scythe.
In Animal Farm, *each animal represents a particular aspect of human nature – greed, cunning, unthinking loyalty, and so on.*

Persuasive language

This is language that is meant to make people agree with a particular idea, or to make them feel something.

Emotive language *is an example. You will find it especially in advertisements, newspaper articles and leaflets.* *(See* **Emotive language***.)*

Phonetic spelling

This is a way of writing words to show how they are being spoken in a particular **accent**.

For example, in a novel, the characters' speech might be written phonetically, as in this extract from The Mayor of Casterbridge, *by Thomas Hardy.*

> *"But no – it cannet be! It cannet! I want to see the warrld!"*

In a poem, a writer might use phonetic spelling to 'write' in their own accent. You need to consider why they have done this. (See **Accent** *and* **Dialect***.)*

Plot

In a story or a novel, this is the order of events – what happens, and when.

Point of view/viewpoint

In a story, we will usually be aware of one character's thoughts and feelings more than others'. This is the viewpoint.

This may be the person telling the story, or it may be another character if the narrator tells us what they see, hear, feel and think. The viewpoint may change during the story. It is worth thinking about viewpoint in poems as well as stories. From whose point of view are we seeing what happens? Whose mind do we get inside?

Pronoun

A pronoun is a word that is used instead of a **noun**.

Examples are "I", "you", "she", "he", "they", "him", "her", "it", "them", "his", "their", "her", "its".

Puns

A pun (or wordplay) is a word that could have more than one meaning.

It might be used in a poem: for example, in this **stanza** *from 'London' by William Blake, the word "mark" means notice as well as a visible mark, drawing attention to both ideas.*

> *"I wander thro' each charter'd street*
> *Near where the charter'd Thames does flow,*
> *And mark in every face I meet*
> *Marks of weakness, marks of woe."*

In newspaper **headlines***, puns are often used to amuse and engage the reader. In* Romeo and Juliet, *Mercutio's dying speech is filled with puns:*

> *"Ask for me tomorrow and you will find me a grave man."*

Reading path

When someone looks at an image, they will probably look at details in a particular order. This is called the reading path.

If you are writing about an image, think about how the reading path may be significant. Does it emphasise certain details? Does it tell a story?

Received pronunciation (RP)

"RP" is an **accent** that is not associated with any particular place.

It used to be known as "BBC English" or "Queen's English". Some people still have a prejudice that it is superior to regional accents.

Register

Register is how formal or informal written text or spoken communication is.

For example, letters and conversations between friends will probably be in an informal register – chatty and full of **slang***. A school report, or a meeting between a parent and a teacher, will be in a more formal register. (See* **Colloquialism** *and* **Slang***.)*

Representation

This is how the subject of a text is made to seem.

For example, a newspaper report may represent teenagers as lazy and ungrateful. A magazine photograph may represent firefighters as strong and heroic.

Think about how details in a text create this effect.

Rhetorical question

Do you really need to be told what this is?

(It's a question which is supposed to have an obvious answer, and is being used to make a point. Look at how they are used in persuasive texts, to encourage the reader to think in the same way as the writer.)

Rhythm

See **Metre**.

Satire

Satire attacks powerful people or ideas, by being funny about them.

For example, comedians often make jokes about politicians. Many writers have attacked the powerful people or ideas of their times by making jokes at their expense. In Hard Times, *Charles Dickens criticised nineteenth-century schools by making them seem absurd.*

Sestet

See **Sonnet**.

Sibilance

The repetition of "s" sounds in writing or speech to create a hissing effect.

In these lines from the play Hamlet, *Shakespeare uses sibilance to bring out Hamlet's disgust at his mother's behaviour:*

> "O, most wicked speed, to post
> With such dexterity to incestuous sheets!"

Simile

This is when something is described by comparing it to something else. When you are writing about a simile, always think about its effect.

For example, "The crowd is like a swarm of wasps" describes how the crowd looks, sounds and moves. It also gives a feeling of danger. Think about the effect you can create with similes in your own writing, too.

A simile is different from a **metaphor**, *because it says that something is like something else, not that it is something else.*

Slang

Slang words are words used by a particular group, usually when they are talking informally.

For example, "bunking off" is slang for truancy; children in different places have lots of other words for it, too. Slang is used in informal speech and writing, and is left out of formal speech and writing. Look at how writers use slang to suggest **mood** *or to create impact. (See* **Colloquialism** *and* **Register**.*)*

Sonnet

This is a particular form of poem, in which there are 14 lines, a regular **rhythm** and a regular rhyme scheme. Sonnets usually have two parts: an eight-line first section, called the **octave**; and a six-line final section, called the **sestet**. They are usually written in **iambic pentameter**.

The sonnet is a form that has been written for hundreds of years, and which is strongly associated with love poetry. The prologue to Romeo and Juliet *is a sonnet. (See* **Metre**.*)*

Standard English

This is a form of English that does not include **slang** or regional **dialect**.

*It follows a set of conventions that some people call "correct" or "proper" English. You should avoid calling it these, as that suggests that there is something "wrong" with dialect or slang. Rather, Standard English is "appropriate" in formal situations. Look for examples of where writers have not used Standard English: why have they done this? (See **Dialect**, **Register** and **Slang**.)*

Stanza

A stanza is a group of lines in a poem, usually following a regular and repeated pattern of **rhythm** and line length.

Stereotype

This is an unfair view of a group of people, which sees them as all the same.

For example, an adult stereotype of teenagers might be that they are rude, aggressive, noisy and selfish.

Amazingly, she turned out to be a stereotypist!

A teenager's stereotype of adults might be that they all live boring, sad and conventional lives. You might find stereotypical descriptions in articles and adverts – of women, of old people or of the police, for example.

Structure

This is the way that a text is ordered or shaped.

*For example, it is how a story begins, develops and ends; it is the order of ideas in a leaflet; or it is the use of **stanzas** or verses in a poem. It is always useful to think about the structure when you are writing about a text of any sort.*

Syllable

Syllables are the separate sounds that make up words. "Go" has one syllable. "Going" has two. "Inexplicable" has five.

When writers use lots of one-syllable (monosyllabic) words, this might help to create a hard, blunt or even angry tone, or a direct simplicity. When they use words with several syllables (polysyllabic), they can create a sense of sophistication, eloquence or technical complexity – like that.

Symbol

This is something that stands for something else.

For example, on a persuasive leaflet, a picture of a candle might be a symbol of hope. In a piece of writing, a flying bird might be symbol of freedom, or fire might come to symbolise aggression and conflict. A reader might find symbolism in something, even if the writer didn't consciously mean it to be there.

Tabloid

Tabloid newspapers (such as the *Sun* and the *Mirror*) usually present news in a brief and easily understood way, trying to make it appeal to as many people as possible. (See **Broadsheet**.)

Text

A text is something that can be read. It could be a book, an image, a film, a **symbol**, a speech, a sign, or a piece of music, or anything else that has meaning for a reader or listener.

Sometimes, the word "text" is used to refer only to words, rather than images or diagrams. Where there is a mixture of these – on a poster or on a Web page, for example – what is called the "text" would usually be just the words.

Theme

This is an idea or topic which is important in a text.

For example, a story might be about the theme of loneliness, growing up, human nature, or friendship. You should be aware of what these are in any literary text, such as a poem, story, play or novel.

Tone

Tone is like **mood**. Just as you can speak in an angry or sad tone of voice, a text can have a tone.

For example, a poem might be reflective or despairing; an advert might be lively or serious; a poster might be angry or accusing. This tone will mainly be created by the choice of words, but lots of other things create tone too – the length of sentences, imagery – even the **layout** *and appearance of the page. (See* **Voice**.*)*

Trochaic tetrameter

See **Metre**.

Verb

A verb is a word which describes an action, such as "build", "destroy", "grow", "think", "say".

Voice

This is a bit like **tone**. If you imagine the writer speaking a text to you, the voice is the tone you imagine them using – the personality behind the text. (See **Tone**.)

9 Reading exam questions

In this chapter, there are examples of the types of questions you might find in each section of the English and English Literature exam papers. The way that the questions are asked or set out changes from year to year, so these are only rough guides.

Students often drop pints by misreading the question…??

These are examples of the questions which you will find in **Section A** of GCSE English (Specification A) Paper 1.

You have no choices

Section A: Reading

- Answer **all** the questions in this Section.
- Spend about **one hour** on this Section.

Read Item 1, the anti-road building leaflet *Murdering our Countryside.*

You are being asked to distinguish between fact and opinion.

1 (a) Choose **three** opinions. Write each one down and explain how you
know each is an opinion and not a fact.

(6 marks)

Read Item 2, the *Observer* **newspaper article 600 million pounds for**
Sorrely bypass

You are now being asked to follow an argument and to select material
appropriate to purpose.

(b) Explain why, according to the writer, the bypass should be built.

(3 marks)

You are now being asked to compare Item 1 *Murdering our Countryside*, **with**
Item 2, the *Observer* **article.**

(c) Compare:

- the points they make
- the way the writers use language to make their points. *(4 marks)*

Annotations (left side):

This means tell
the difference

This is what the
examiner is
looking for

You need to show
that you understand
the argument

You need to show
that you understand
how types of writing
are different

'Points' include ideas
and messages

Annotations (right side):

This means
quote exactly

You must
give reasons

Quote and refer to details
to support your ideas

Quote and refer to
specific examples

110

You are now being asked to read Item 3, the front page of the *Sorrely Weekly News* and Items 1 and 2 as media texts.

2 (a) Comment on the ways meanings are conveyed in words and images in
        Item 1, *Murdering our Countryside*.
                                                                    (4 marks)

   (b) How do the form, layout and presentation of **Item 2**, the article from
        the *Observer* support the writer's argument?
                                                                    (4 marks)

   (c) Compare the way **Item 2** and **Item 3**, the two newspaper articles,
        present the story of the bypass to their different audiences.

        You should comment on:

        • the purpose of each article

        • the language used in each

        • the use of images.
                                                                    (6 marks)

This is about how
images and layout
work together with
the words

You will be expected to write
about images and layout, as well
as the words, and how all of
these may affect audiences

111

These are examples of the questions which you will find in **Section B** of **GCSE English (Specification A) Paper 1**.

Section B: Writing to Argue, Persuade or Advise

- Answer **one** question from this Section.

Choose carefully

- You may use some of the information from Section A if you want to, but you do not have to do so. If you use any of the information, <u>do not simply copy it.</u>

This is important

- Spend about **45 minutes** on this Section.

Remember:

- Spend 5 minutes planning and sequencing your material

This means putting your ideas or points in order

- You should write about two sides in your answer book

You may well write more, especially if you have large handwriting

- Spend 5 minutes checking:
  - your paragraphing
  - your punctuation
  - your spelling.

Either

3 You live in a town near to a planned new motorway. Write a letter to the local newspaper in which you argue either for or against the building of this new road.

This would be printed in the newspaper, for its readers to see

This is the key word

(*27 marks*)

112

Or

The audience is very important. Your writing must be aimed at it

4 Write a speech for a local public meeting where you, as a school student, try to

persuade the council to build one of the following:

- a new skate park
- a swimming pool
- a play park for young children.

Remember to:

Keep to the point

- write as yourself
- concentrate on your chosen issue
- use persuasive language
- write in an appropriate style for a speech.

(27 marks)

This is the key word

Or

5 A group of students from your school is planning a protest against a proposed new road. Write detailed **advice** on how best to do this.

You should include:

- the sort of event that will work well
- how to plan the event
- problems that might arise and how to avoid them.

(27 marks)

This is the key word

If there are bullets, use them to help you to organise your writing

Or

Make sure your writing is appropriate to the context and audience

6 Write an article for a tabloid newspaper in which you:

argue that conserving wildlife is more important than building new roads

and **persuade** the reader to agree with you.

(27 marks)

One question will ask you to combine two kinds of writing

113

This is an example of the question on writing to inform, explain or describe of the type that you might find in **Section B** of **GCSE English (Specification A) Paper 2.**

Section B: Writing to Inform, Explain or Describe

- Answer **one** question from this Section.
- Spend about **45 minutes** on this Section.

Remember:

- Spend 5 minutes planning and sequencing your material

  > This means putting your ideas or points in order

- Try to write at least one side in your answer book

  > You may well write more, especially if you have large handwriting

- Spend 5 minutes checking:
  - your paragraphing
  - your punctuation
  - your spelling.

Either

2 Your school asks you to help with its exchange programme with its French partner school. You are asked to write a short introduction to your school for the French students, in the form of a letter, informing them of important facts which they will find helpful on their visit.

> informing — This is the key word. You are trying to get information across as clearly as possible

> The French students — The audience is very important. Your writing must be aimed at it

Write the letter.

(27 marks)

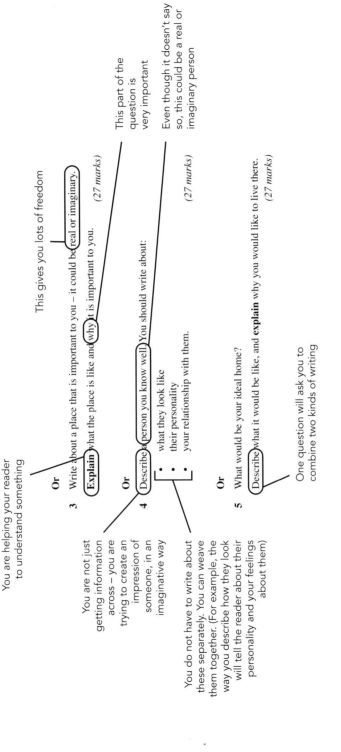

You are not just describing it. You are helping your reader to understand something

This gives you lots of freedom

This part of the question is very important

Even though it doesn't say so, this could be a real or imaginary person

Or

3   Write about a place that is important to you – it could be real or imaginary. **Explain** what the place is like and why it is important to you.   *(27 marks)*

Or

4   Describe a person you know well. You should write about:

- what they look like
- their personality
- your relationship with them.

  (27 marks)

Or

5   What would be your ideal home? Describe what it would be like, and **explain** why you would like to live there.   *(27 marks)*

You are not just getting information across – you are trying to create an impression of someone, in an imaginative way

You do not have to write about these separately. You can weave them together. (For example, the way you describe how they look will tell the reader about their personality and your feelings about them)

One question will ask you to combine two kinds of writing

115

This is an example of a question on pre-1914 and post-1914 poetry, which you will find in **Section B** of the **GCSE English Literature (Specification A) paper.**

Section B: Pre-1914 and Post-1914 Poetry

- Answer **one** question from this Section.

- You should spend about **one hour** on this Section.

- Each question carries 36 marks.

The following questions refer to the *Literature* section of your AQA Anthology that you have been using during the course.

In your answer you **must** refer to pre-1914 poems **and** post-1914 poems.

This is very important

Carol Ann Duffy and Simon Armitage

Either

23 Compare how relationships which have gone wrong are shown in 'My Last Duchess' by Robert Browning and three other poems – one pre-1914 poem, one by Carol Ann Duffy, and one by Simon Armitage.

Make sure you are writing about the right poems

(36 marks)

What is similar and what is different?

Or

24 (a) Compare how Carol Ann Duffy and Simon Armitage present characters in 'Stealing' and 'Hitcher'.

(b) Compare these poems with any two in the pre-1914 Poetry Bank.

(36 marks)

Remember to compare:
- the characters the poets write about.
- the methods the poets use to present the characters.

Or

25 (a) Compare how violence is presented in 'Education for Leisure' by Carol Ann Duffy and 'The Laboratory' by Robert Browning.

(b) Compare these poems with two more poems, one by Simon Armitage and one from the pre-1914 Poetry Bank.

(36 marks)

This means describe or give an impression of

Some questions may have bullets. If so, use them to plan your answer

Make sure that you choose poems which fit the question

This is asking you to comment on the language and the writer's techniques

117

This is an example of a question on 'Poems from different cultures and traditions', of the type that you might find in **Section A** of **GCSE English (Specification A) Paper 2.**

Section A: Poetry from different cultures and traditions

Either

1 Compare the ways in which the poets present places in 'Nothing's Changed' and **one** other poem from the 'Poems from different cultures and traditions'.

Write about:

- what the different places are like
- what the poets feel about them
- how the language brings out what the places are like
- how the language shows what the poets think about the places
- which poem you prefer and why.

(27 marks)

Or

2 Compare 'Half Caste' with one other poem, showing how the poets reveal their feelings about who they are.

Write about:

- their ideas about who they are
- what they feel about who they are
- the methods they use to reveal their ideas and feelings.

(27 marks)

Annotations (handwritten/marginal notes):

- Don't just write about the poems separately
- Always quote and refer to details in the poems
- Give reasons for your choice
- Remember to quote examples of the writers' uses of language
- This includes reading between the lines

This is an example of a question on a novel of the type that you might find in **Section A** of the **English Literature Paper**. Even if you are not revising a novel, it will give you useful hints about how to read questions.

Questions often use a quotation from the text as a starting point. This is designed to help you focus on a particular aspect or part of the text. It is important to look for key words in the quotation to refer to in your answer

Sums up or develops

William Golding: *Lord of the Flies*

Themes are ideas or topics which the text explores

This means most important

4   At the end of the novel Ralph is described as weeping for "the end of innocence, the darkness of man's heart".

Consider how the ending of *Lord of the Flies* reflects the central themes of the novel.

You should write about:

what you believe are the writer's main concerns and ideas in the novel

how these are conveyed to the reader in the final pages

your response to the ending.

(36 marks)

Communicated or put across

The themes the writer has been exploring through the events of the novel and the actions of the characters, or questions and ideas that the writer is putting forward

This invites you to think about and explain what you know and to take it on into new areas

Your thoughts and feelings, supported if necessary by evidence (quotations, reference to specific events, etc)

This is an example of a question on short stories of the type that you might find in **Section A** of the **GCSE English Literature (Specification A) Paper**. Even if you are not revising short stories, it will give you useful hints about how to read questions.

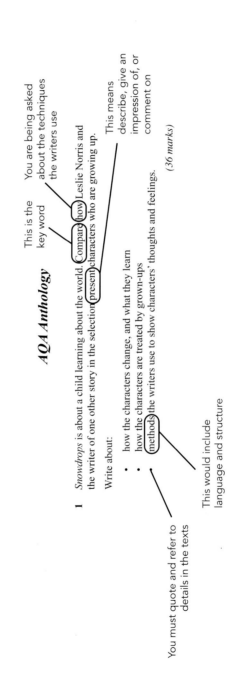

AQA Anthology

This is the key word

You are being asked about the techniques the writers use

1 *Snowdrops* is about a child learning about the world. Compare how Leslie Norris and the writer of one other story in the selection present characters who are growing up.

This means describe, give an impression of, or comment on

Write about:

• how the characters change, and what they learn
• how the characters are treated by grown-ups

methods the writers use to show characters' thoughts and feelings.

This would include language and structure

(36 marks)

You must quote and refer to details in the texts

120